# CLOSE THE
# BACK DOOR

# CLOSE THE BACK DOOR

## Ways to Create a Caring Congregational Fellowship

**Alan F. Harre**

Publishing House
St. Louis

Copyright 1984 Concordia Publishing House
3558 S. Jefferson Avenue, St. Louis, MO 63118
Manufactured in the United States of America

---

Library of Congress Cataloging in Publication Data

Harre, Alan F.
    Close the back door.

    (Speaking the Gospel series)
    1. Ex.-church members. I. Title. II. Title: Close the back door. III. Series.
BV820.H34 1984        254'.5        83-27281
ISBN 0-570-03932-0 (pbk.)

---

3  4  5  6  7  8  9  10  MAL  93  92  91  90  89  88  87  86  85

# Contents

# Introduction

Conscientious pastors and committed lay members of Christian congregations often find themselves reflecting on the subject of inactive members and how best to cope with individuals who drop out of active participation in the programs and worship life of a local parish. Denominational executives discover that these concerns appear with regularity on the agendas of meetings they are called upon to attend. Every congregation and denomination is painfully aware of how many of their constituents have become or are becoming inactive. It has been estimated that the Protestant churches of the United States remove from membership rosters or place on inactive lists over two million persons every year.[1] This estimate does not include all those people who have become inactive but whose names remain on membership rosters until they die.

This reality has led to all manner of advice-giving, handwringing, congregational resolutions to "clean out the deadwood," and exhortations that congregational leaders do a better job of soul care. In addition, social scientists, particularly sociologists of religion and denominational executives charged with the responsibilities to do statistical research, have conducted numerous empirical research studies on the subjects of inactive members, the unchurched, denominational switchers, and church growth.

The findings of these empirical studies are generally not employed by parish clergy and lay leaders. Perhaps the primary reason for this is that most parish leaders do not read the technical journals which publish the research reports. Even if parish leaders read the journals, they might be a bit frustrated in trying to make use of the results of the studies. Most parish leaders have little or no knowledge of (1) the nature of the intellectual structures or models employed by social scientists, (2) statistical analysis, and (3) how one goes about evaluating the relative importance of the results of a given study in relationship to the findings of other studies which have investigated the same or similar subjects. One of the great gifts of Lyle Schaller is that he has been popularizing and making understandable the findings of other social scientists for many years. One of the purposes of this volume is to interpret and explain what social scientists have learned about people who have become or are becoming church dropouts.

The writer has a number of biases about which he is acutely aware. It is important that the reader take these biases into consideration as he works through the materials that follow.

In the first place, the writer believes that it is imperative for the individual congregation to have as its primary motivation the desire to demonstrate by its every action and reaction that it is a functioning part of the body of Christ. As a portion of the body of Christ here on earth, the congregation is called upon to live out every aspect of its corporate life in agreement with what it claims to be. Such agreement is perceived by members and nonmembers as a sign of integrity and genuineness. Without such agreement the entire witness of the congregation is blunted.

Second, the individual congregation has the responsibility to share the Good News of Jesus Christ with all who are outside the faith and to invite them to affiliate with that congregation in worship, service, fellowship, nurture, and "good-newsing" additional people. These activities have as one of their purposes the "discipling" of members of the congregations so that, as the Holy Spirit ministers to them through Word and sacraments, they might grow to spiritual maturity. One hoped-for manifestation of such spiritual maturity is that these individuals would not forsake their Lord by drifting into apostasy.

It is imperative that congregations do not automatically assume that when members have become dropouts from the congregation's life they have also rejected their Lord and become apostate. The prejudgment that someone has become apostate must take into consideration other variables, all of which are suggested in the Bible, rather than just the variable of participation in the life of a local congregation. As Lyle Schaller has written, "There does not appear to be any positive correlation between the commitment of the individual to Jesus Christ as Lord and Savior and the loyalty of that particular individual to a certain congregation. . . . A loyalty to Jesus Christ does not automatically keep people in a specific parish."[2]

Third, as the individual congregation goes about its task of "good-newsing" persons who are not Christians and "discipling" members, the power of God is brought to bear on all such people through the Gospel. The term "Gospel" is here used in its technical, narrow Lutheran sense of "Gospel" as juxtaposed to "Law." When a congregation promotes membership on the basis of considerations like its success, the social class of its members, its clever programming, and a variety of other claims to fame, that congregation is communicating a gospel of cheap grace much more reminiscent of the way of the world and its standards than of the costly grace which undergirds the Gospel message.

The writer also has some undergirding assumptions that he employs which are important to reveal. The initial assumption is that most pastors and lay persons prefer to avoid ministering to individuals who have become inactive. Many other congregational tasks are perceived to be more attractive and exciting than visiting and attempting to reclaim inactive members. As a result of this attitude, pastors and lay leaders put off calling on inactive members. When feelings of guilt arise over ignoring these people, manifold rationalizations, including the importance of gaining new members, help to give comfort to troubled consciences.

A second assumption is that stereotypes which have developed over the years concerning the character and motivations of members who have become inactive are generally far too simplistic. Such people do not comprise a homogeneous grouping of people. They are not motivated by a limited number of causes to become church dropouts. Rather, specific individuals are motivated to inactivity by a wide variety of concerns, factors, conditions, and situations.

A third assumption is that most congregations elect or appoint their most talented members to positions which are designed to meet the survival goals of the congregation. Such survival goals include the raising of money and keeping the physical facilities of the congregation in good repair. This practice leaves less talented and perhaps less committed members of the congregation for managing the committees, boards, and agencies that are responsible for evangelism, soul care, and the "discipling" of the congregation's members.

A fourth assumption is that people learn to be religious. The primary teachers of religious attitudes are parents and spouses. This learning can be enhanced or decreased by things like doctrinal beliefs, attitudes about sexual matters, feelings about the clergy serving local congregations, and the sermons that are delivered at worship services. However, the primary socialization force to encourage church participation and other religious behavior remains the family. Of most importance to individuals is the attitude and behavior of the spouse in a family constellation.[3] By implication this means that other variables which are used in many empirical studies will be much less powerful and profound predictors of religious behaviors like church attendance.

A fifth assumption is that trends in the percentage of people who participate in church life vary greatly over even short periods of time. Therefore it is very hazardous to try to predict what will happen from one decade to the next.[4]

A responsible analysis of the subject of inactive members cannot be presented without taking seriously the contributions of numerous social scientists who have conducted a multitude of studies on this and related subjects. Yet, as asserted earlier, most parish leaders are relatively unsophisticated in regard to the processes of conducting social science research and how to make use of the conclusions arrived at on the basis of the data collected and analyzed. Prior to reporting on some important findings of various social scientists relative to the issue of becoming inactive in the local congregation, it is important that the reader be aware of the major difficulties that are inherent in designing and carrying out research efforts in the area of human behaviors and attitudes and in applying the conclusions that have been drawn from the the data generated by such studies.

Among the difficulties faced by social scientists is that people change continually—to some degree day in and day out. This is the primary reason why pollsters take their polls right up to and during an election. They know how volatile and fickle the attitudes and intentions of some people can be. Thus every empirical study is merely a snapshot of the variety of opinions, beliefs, attitudes, and behaviors of a randomly identified group of people on the day they were interviewed.

Even such a snapshot is tentative because we can only say that the people who completed questionnaires *may* have held a particular set of beliefs, opinions, or attitudes and *may* have been willing to exhibit behavior consistent with those beliefs, opinions, and attitudes. An empirical study is not a motion picture but a single snapshot. These limitations cannot be stressed too strongly.

The assertion above that the data gathered in empirical studies *may* reflect the attitudes, beliefs, or opinions of a sample of people on a given day about a particular subject further emphasizes the tentativeness of all data. Another significant problem faced by researchers in the social sciences is that respondents can choose to lie to the interviewer or give inaccurate data as they complete a paper-and-pencil instrument. People may provide such less-than-accurate information for a variety of reasons. Perhaps they want to please the interviewer. Or they may want to present themselves in a particular way. Many subjects are test- or instrument-wise enough to "see through" the instrument. In other words, such subjects determine what it is the researcher is attempting to find, and they consciously or unconsciously set out to deceive him or to provide him with what they perceive he wants even though they are providing false information in the process.

A third problem revolves around the use of language. There is always the possibility that items the researcher has designed so carefully can be misunderstood by those who respond. This is a significant problem that social scientists try to prevent by carefully field-testing the instrument prior to using it, yet there is no way to make absolutely certain that all respondents will perfectly understand what they are being asked in a particular question.

A fourth problem is the fact that when one is doing research on human beings there is usually a maddening multiplicity of independent variables. If these independent variables cannot be held constant or if the researcher does not recognize that they are important, the data one gathers may be a proverbial comparison of apples and oranges. For example, a criticism that has been leveled at Dean Kelley's methodology in the preparation of his famous book *Why Conservative Churches Are Growing* is that if Kelley had held constant the fertility rates in the various denominations he compared, much of the data he discovered to be statistically significant would not have been so any longer.

It is not scholarly to put together a research design to look for whatever it is that the researcher may find. Research that is worthy of the title "scholarly research" must be based on some theoretical model. Most people are more aware of theoretical models in the natural sciences (i. e., Einstein's theory of relativity, the theory of evolution, etc.) than they are of the theoretical models employed in the social sciences. Yet there are hundreds and perhaps even thousands of theoretical models that are being used in all the social sciences each day. Thus in the best of all worlds the social scientist evaluates a wide variety of specific theoretical models and the particular insights that each model might produce before selecting a model he will employ in his new effort of empirical research.

Andrew Greeley is very critical of the scientific models sociologists of religion have used over the past decades. In his book *Crisis in the Church* Greeley writes: "Secularization, social class, relevance, then, simply are not even remotely adequate explanations of American religious affiliation and disaffiliation. The socialization model, foreshadowed by John Kotre and clearly enunciated by William McCready, is vastly more useful in approaching the phenomenon of American religion."[5]

At some time in the future some other sociologist may be as critical of the "socialization model" as Greeley is critical of the models that emphasize "secularization," "social class," and "relevance."

Another important factor that must be considered is that a research design, since it is based on a specific theoretical model, will ask questions only in one way. How a question is asked will cause a social scientist to arrive at a particular answer to the question. Kelley's question, "Does the variable of the theological orientation of given denominations help to identify which denominations are growing and which denominations have ceased growing?" calls upon the social scientist to gather different data and facts and to evaluate those data and facts differently as he attempts to answer the question than does the question, "Does the fertility rate of the members of specific denominations help to identify which denominations are growing and which denominations have ceased to grow?" Therefore the selection of a theoretical model and the questions the model will cause the researcher to ask have profound implications on what conclusions the research effort will generate. As was said in the rural America of the 1920s and 1930s, "Select your ruts carefully, for you will be in them a long time."

In other words, a theoretical model is a set of intellectual ruts. The theoretical model determines the questions asked, the data that must be gathered, and predetermines the answers that will be forthcoming at the conclusion of the research effort.

Assuming that a social scientist has (1) chosen the theoretical model carefully, (2) conducted the research project with integrity, (3) taken into consideration all the germane variables, and (4) evaluated the gathered data properly, there is still one more issue, which is the most important consideration of all. This consideration is that findings of social scientific research are properly used if they are perceived as descriptive and improperly used if they are assumed to be prescriptive.

A case in point, familiar to almost every adult in the United States, is what the judicial branch of the federal government has done with the conclusions of Dr. James S. Coleman's 1966 report entitled "Equality of Educational Opportunity."

The data gathered by Dr. Coleman, prior to writing his now famous report, were interpreted as demonstrating that poor black children achieved at a higher level in school if they were able to attend classes with white middle-class students. Coleman's report described a situation that seemed generally to be the case from a statistical vantage point.

If Dr. Coleman's report had been duly filed, shelved, and ignored, as is the fate of so many studies, his work would probably have been cited only in footnotes of Ph.D. and Ed.D. dissertations, and some other sociologists might have made attempts to see if they could repeat his findings.

However, this was not the fate of Coleman's report. Its contents began to be used by federal judges to mandate school desegregation by means of a process which came to be called "busing." When this happened, Coleman's study was no longer a descriptive report by a well-known sociologist of what he had discovered relative to the classroom achievement of black, lowerclass children. The conclusions of the study began to be employed prescriptively by the courts and were used to justify the actions and judgments of the judges. Thus the application of the conclusions of the Coleman report became the principal battleground between the ideologies of political liberals and conservatives. Court actions justified by citing Coleman's conclusions were condemned by white supremacists and black supremacists, while white and black moderates hailed the courts' actions as the beginning of a new day of significant federal involvement in the area of civil rights.

This lesson from recent history illustrates a number of basic points. The first is that there is a significant difference between descriptive and prescriptive applications of conclusions reached through social science research. Second, when descriptive conclusions are used prescriptively, such applications will create ideological conflicts. Third, since every human being has ideological commitments, there is a very great likelihood that individuals will read, study, and apply only those studies whose conclusions seem to agree with their own prior ideological commitments. Fourth, because of this propensity of human beings to accept and integrate only those conclusions which are congruent with commitments and understandings already held, there is a danger that causal factors will be perceived too simplistically and important con-siderations will be ignored because they conflict with ideological commitments. Finally, simplistic understandings cause people to design superficial plans to confront problems which are too complex to remedy with such easy approaches. Failure of these superficial plans makes people even more reticent to make a second attempt at confronting the issue.

All of the above has been written by way of warning to the reader. The material that follows attempts to paint the mosaic of inactive members from many vantage points. The reader will not find a simple "cookbook" approach to confronting the people who have become inactive. Rather the reader will discover a multiplicity of ways to understand who the inactive people are, why they were motivated to become inactive, and numerous ways the various types of inactive people might be approached. To select only those causes that conform to ideology and personal experience or which seem easiest to adress will likely produce frustration and cynicism over the long haul. Openness and willingness to seriously consider all the possibilities will be more likely to produce effective strategies. Openness to the data will also reflect willingness to follow through on the implications of the time-worn cliche, "You've got to meet people where they are."

# Chapter 1

# Who Are the Dropouts?

Before any strategy can be developed to try to reclaim inactive members for parish life, it is necessary to know what kinds or types of people drop out. It is imperative to perceive the variety of motivations which nudge people into a posture of inactivity. As will soon become evident from the variety of factors described later in this chapter, the answer to the question "Who are the inactive?" is complex and calls for a complex answer.

At the outset it is important to acknowledge that the data collected on why people are inactive is problematic in that it is always gathered *ex post facto*. There seems to be no data that reflects a longitudinal approach to determining how church members function month in and month out and what elements impinge on them as time passes to cause them to contemplate, begin, and complete the process of dropping out. Because of this reality all findings must be weighed carefully. The data supplied by the dropouts reflects the way they feel when they are being interviewed. They may choose to be less than candid in their responses. They may answer the questions in ways that seek to justify their actions. They may have lost touch with important considerations because of the passing of time. In short, the data is not as "hard" as we would like it to be. The reader needs to keep this reality in mind when proceeding to study the materials that follow.

Hale's vantage point is helpful here. He has written: "The rites of passage by which people become members of religious communities are well known. The rites of passage by which people leave, the 'tipping phenomenon,' remains unexplored."[1]

Hale's technique of interviewing unchurched people provided him with much anecdotal material. In summarizing his material, he wrote:

"The anecdotal material collected in this study reports the perspectives people have of the world we call 'church.' All the stories have in common a singular behavioral result: namely, separation from the religious institutions of our society. . . . We do not know precisely what triggers the exodus for some and what holds others in. The indications seem to suggest that for most the process of estrangement is gradual."[2]

As social scientists have studied the issues of promoting participation and intervening in the lives of individuals who drop out of a congregation's life, four major categories summarize the various factors that seem to be important. These categories are (1) national contextual factors, (2) national institutional factors, (3) local contextual factors, and (4) local institutional factors. A local congregation has no power to influence national contextual factors, little or no power to influence national institutional and local contextual factors. The local congregation can only influence and intentionally shape local institutional factors.[3]

Inherent in these categories are the seeds of significant intellectual debates and conflicts produced by ideological commitments. For example, some like H. Paul Douglass have argued that the local congregation and its "success" is almost totally dependent on local contextual factors. Other writers such as McGavran, Wagner, and Kelley emphasize the importance of local institutional factors. More recent studies suggest that both sets of factors contribute to a congregation's "success" or decline. The specific percentage of each factor's contribution is highly dependent on the specifics of a given situation.[4]

It is also important to note that there has been a great deal of similarity in the patterns of the large denominations concerning dropouts from their local congregations. Because of this similarity in patterns some argue that national contextual factors are much more important than national institutional (denominational) factors in explaining what has happened.[5]

Some of the data reflected in this chapter suggest that many of the reasons why individuals drop out of the life of a local congregation are beyond the congregation's control and power. A sense of frustration could result as that awareness becomes more sharply focused. On the other hand, there are other factors that clearly can be addressed by the local congregation. Rather than despairing over the unattainable, it would appear to be prudent to concentrate efforts on addressing those areas where the congregation is capable of positive and remedial action.

Using data generated by the 1978 Gallup study, Roozen has concluded that about 40 percent of the American population is unchurched. Over 90 percent of these unchurched Americans were at one time or another in their lifetime affiliated in some sense with a religious community. Over 60 percent of the nonchurched people reported having attended church regularly or participated in religious instruction classes earlier in their lifetime.[6]

Roozen has also concluded that almost 50 percent of Americans drop out of active religious participation at some point during their lifetime.[7] This percentage demonstrates how pervasive the issue of dropouts is for church leaders. To place these statistics in the proper context it is imperative to add that many of these people return to church life later in their lifetime. Roozen suggests that up to 80 percent return to church.[8]

Roozen has also asserted that in the 1970s reentry rates of dropouts have risen so that now reentries offset the losses incurred by dropouts. For the first time in 50 years the two rates are in balance.[9] Much more will be said later about the returnees and what factors seem to motivate their return.

A relatively consistent finding of studies is that the age variable is important in evaluating the percentage of members who drop out of churches. However, recent studies have called into question some results of studies conducted earlier. Roozen discovered that among preteen children there is a very low dropout rate. However, the dropout rate increases significantly during the teen years.[10]

Numerous suggestions have been offered to explain this rise in the rate of dropouts among teenagers. Perhaps the increased attrition rate reflects the fact that parents have less influence on teenagers than they do on preteen children. It is also possible that teenagers perceive the church as having little of worth to offer them as individuals. Some have hypothesized that the conventional church program caters to the needs of preteen children and adults. Thus the church is perceived as having little of relevance to offer the average teenager. This withdrawal from the church has been noted particularly among males, those individuals who have graduated from high school, those who have gotten a college education, and those who have come from Roman Catholic backgrounds.[11]

Once the respondents mature beyond the teen years and reach the early 20s the dropout rate decreases by almost one-half from the rate found among teenagers. Respondents in their late 20s and early 30s have an attrition rate of one-half that of the respondents who are teenagers. This decrease in the dropout rate remains about the same for respondents until they reach the mid-50s. In the mid-50s the dropout rate is about half the rate of dropouts of people in the late 30s through the mid-50s.[12]

Roozen summarizes his findings in these words: "The likelihood of pre-teen disengagement is slight (2.6 percent); the dropout rate reaches its maximum among teens (15.5 percent); drops for those in their early twenties to 9.1 percent; plateaus at around 4.6 percent for those twenty-five to fifty-four; then drops to pre-teen levels for those over fifty-five."[13]

It should be noted that these data disagree with those collected earlier by various social scientists. Earlier studies reported a continued increase in the dropout rate from church membership among individuals from the teen years into early adulthood and among those who had become older adults or elderly.[14]

The data from various studies strongly imply that individuals who have chosen to become inactive from organized church life are those whose lives reflect cosmopolitan attitudes and life-styles. Individuals who have finished high school are twice as likely to drop out as those who did not graduate from high school. It appears that as people become better educated they are likely to be more mobile, more diversified in their value systems, and less likely to remain under the influence of a single local congregation and a nuclear or extended family.[15]

Although the above statements are generally accurate, the picture is even more complex than has been suggested. The changes that have come about in commitment to the church have been greatly affected by the religious climate on a national scale. This climate change is part of a larger mosaic of value changes. These changes cluster around values like "sex and family, birth control, ideal family size, civil liberties, legalization of marijuana and (among Catholics) political party identification."[16]

Hoge judges that all these changes have been in the "direction of individualism, personal freedom and tolerance of diversity."[17] This new attitude has been adopted most enthusiastically by young adults, particularly college-educated young adults. This change has taken place since 1960—which explains why reports of studies conducted before then asserted that college-educated adults were more likely to be church attenders than the non-college-educated population.[18] Thus the national contextual factor of, for lack of a better term, "secularization" is primarily responsible for the disaffiliation of college students and college graduates from the institutional church.

Roozen offers the hopeful prognosis that most teenage dropouts will return to active church involvement sometime later in their lives. He suggests that the return rate is particularly high for individuals in their late 20s and early 30s, and for those who perceived religion to be very important during their childhood.[19]

Studies conducted on individuals who have matured beyond their teen years have produced a variety of findings. In some studies the most frequently mentioned reason for dropping out was that the subjects did not feel they were loved, accepted, or wanted by other members of the congregation. Their perception was that no one in the congregation was demonstrating any real love or concern for them.[20]

In other studies specific events which disrupted the lives of the subjects were cited as the primary reasons for dropping out of active church life. The reason most often identified by those 20 to 54 years of age was moving to a new community. After age 54 poor health became the reason identified most frequently. In many instances these disruptions in life cause subjects to pinpoint other items like irrelevance of the church and conflict with the church or a church member as additional causes for dropping out.[21]

Studies have also listed personal considerations such as "illness in the family, changes in work schedules, transportation problems, lack of support or opposition from other family members, too busy with other responsibilities, and leisure pursuits . . ." as important reasons why respondents have dropped out of church.[22]

Hartman reported that the cluster of reasons cited third-most-frequently was that the activites of the church and church school were not relevant. Respondents identified such things as "poor sermons or teaching, too much boredom and busywork, irrelevant curriculum resources, and apathy among church workers."[23]

Dr. John Savage of L.E.A.D. Consultants of Pittsford, N. Y., has popularized through his book *The Bored and Apathetic Church Member* and his cassette tapes a relatively simple typology of why people drop out of the church. Savage designed his study using a theoretical model which emphasizes the "Anxiety-Anger Complex."[24] Savage assumed that people move away from the church when their life in the church produces some kind of anxiety.[25] This is a significant assumption to make. Savage worked with four types of anxiety: (1) reality, (2) neurotic, (3) moral, and (4) existential.[26]

After interviewing 101 New York Methodists representing four congregations who had been categorized in three groupings as very active members, less active members, and inactive members, Savage developed a typology which asserts that the primary motivations people have for dropping out of church come from their participation in the church itself. All of the 23 dropouts had had an anxiety-provoking event happen to them. Frequently conflicts with one or more of a cluster of persons (pastor, church member, family member) or the feeling of being overworked in the church's organizational life constituted the anxiety-provoking event. This event was reacted to by the subject in anger. If the person turned the blame inward, the person ultimately became a bored church member and dropped out. If the person turned the blame outward, he became an apathetic member and also dropped out of church life.[27]

Savage found that all 23 respondents asserted that no one had ever come to visit them to find out why they dropped out. This fact made the subjects bitter. They felt that this lack of action on the part of the leaders of the congregation confirmed the fact that no one in their congregation really cared about them.

One highly emotionally charged finding of Savage is that dropouts consciously or unconsciously give the local congregation only six to eight weeks once they have dropped out to call on them. If the subjects did not receive some indication they were missed in that period of time, they reinvested their efforts in other pursuits.[28]

Therefore, according to Savage, people are motivated to remain members of congregations or drop out of congregations because of factors stemming from their participation in those congregations. When members of congregations feel positive about their experiences in the congregation, when they feel appreciated and loved, they will become more and more involved in the life of the congregation. But if they later begin to feel that they are being rejected, that they are no longer appreciated and loved as much as they were in the past, then they are likely to experience feelings of anger, disillusionment, and finally grief, and they drop out.[29] This may also explain why some dropouts describe themselves as having been overworked. Such people feel as if their strength and energy has been used up by the church.[30]

Savage's typology is reminiscent of a cartoon published orginally in the *New Yorker* magazine. It pictures an older male, walking along in a slouched position, hands in overcoat pockets, with an unhappy look on his face. In a circle around the individual are the following words written in this order "awareness—involvement—activism—confrontation—disenchantment—alienation—apathy."[31]

William McKinney has described such dropouts as the disenchanted. He describes the disenchanted as "the reactive dropouts, those who covet church relationships but for whom church experiences have been so unsatisfactory or painful that they stay outside."[32]

Walrath and others have judged that Savage's typology represents a small percentage of the people who drop out of congregations. These types of dropouts are obviously going to be noticed because "they have turned their backs on the church." If this judgment is accurate, to design a reclamation program for dropouts assuming only Savage's model will not effectively minister to the large percentage of dropouts whose reasons for leaving are widely divergent and more complex than provided for in Savage's model.[33]

Numbers of analysts have highlighted the importance of spouse and family for enhancing or diminishing the involvement of individuals in the life of the church. Probably no sociologist has been more adamant about this factor than Andrew Greeley. He has written: "It is the family of procreation, the family in which one participates as a husband or wife, that really matters. In most cases that family accounts for more of the variance in religious behavior than all the other variables put together."[34]

In this quotation Greeley is asserting that all the other variables social scientists are fond of investigating (education, social class, race, denominational affiliation, areas of the country in which respondents live, etc.) are less important as predictors of religious affiliation than the "family of procreation."

Greeley has reported that as marital satisfaction increases there seems to be an increasing closeness to the church. Positive influence toward religious commitment on the part of a spouse is most influential in satisfying marriages. And in satisfying marriages the influence of the spouse tends to lean in the direction of greater religiousness.[35] Thus Greeley proposes, "Improve the quality of marital intimacy and very likely the level of religious devotion will rise."[36] Later he says, "When religious leaders, journalists and theorists raise the question, 'How do you make people more religious?' the best answer that can be offered on the basis of this volume is 'make marriages happier.' "[37]

In light of the above statements relative to the importance of a spouse's religious commitment for the other spouse's involvement in the life of the church, it is not surprising that a number of authors have commented on the negative effects of religiously mixed marriages. People often become inactive after they have joined their spouse's denomination or congregation.[38] Others begin to drift toward dropping out when they discover that their spouse is not supportive of their involvement in or commitment to the church.[39]

The importance of the family climate and religious commitment is not limited to husband-and-wife relationships. Greeley has also reported that family tensions during childhood have a negative effect on the religiousness of people as they become adults. Childhood family tensions seem to cause people to view the church in a negative manner.[40]

Hunsberger, using 51 control subjects and 51 apostate subjects, discovered supporting evidence for Greeley's assertions. Hunsberger summarized his conclusions by writing: "Emphasis on religion in childhood is positively associated with later religiosity and agreement with parental religious teachings. Thus it is suggested that the religious environment of the home also may play an important part in the apostasy process, such that weaker emphasis on religion and religious practice is related to greater probability of apostasy later in life."[41]

Savage's findings, reported above, included the fact that conflicts with family members were major contributors to triggering his subjects' anxiety, anger, apathy, boredom, and dropping-out pattern.

In 1965 Donald Metz reported that his interviews of attending and nonattending members of two Methodist congregations produced the results that almost one-fourth of the inactive members of these congregations cited some family difficulty as their primary reason for being nonattenders. Within this primary reason there were two major subreasons for the inactivity. One subgroup indicated that their spouses were not interested in church. The second subreason was that there had been some change in regard to children.[42] The very limited study done by Vangerud on inactive members of one congregation caused him to conclude: "Withdrawal from corporate worship in most cases seemed to be a coping device designed to reestablish a new balance in the family constellation."[43]

The assertion that parental religious teaching is influential in the lives of children needs to be clarified lest it be misunderstood. Roozen found that people who had been raised by conservative Protestant mothers were the most likely to drop out of the life of the church. The dropout rate of teenagers was the highest for those with conservative Protestant backgrounds. The dropout rate of teens and young adults among Catholics and liberal Protestants is more evenly divided between individuals in their teens and individuals in their early 20s than is the case with conservative Protestants. In general the dropout rate is lower for teens and young adults who felt religion was very important to them during their childhood. But even among those who perceived religion to be very important during their childhood, 20 percent were no longer active church participants by the age of 25.[44]

It has become clear that, although they do not often admit it, one of the primary motivations people have for joining congregations is the relationships they have established or want to establish with others. Since social satisfaction and social needs are motivators for affiliation, it is logical to conclude that people drop out of congregations when their social relationships are destroyed or when the relationships do not meet the members' initial expectations. The leaders of growing congregations have recognized and attempted to meet the needs of members for (1) recognition, (2) esteem, and (3) a sense of belonging.[45] Dudley reports that the dropouts who remain within the vicinity of their former congregation most often cite broken relationships as the major reason for dropping out of church. Some former Presbyterians listed the loss of significant friendships as the most important reason for leaving their church.[46]

Donald Metz has also pointed to the importance of troubled relationships as a motivator of people who dropped out of churches. Metz reported that one of the major criticisms that nonattenders had concerning their two local Methodist congregations was the lack of personal contacts they had with fellow congregational members.[47]

Further evidence of the importance of good personal relationships as motivators for involvement in the life of a congregation and broken or poor personal relationships as motivators for dropping out of congregations is found in other studies. A United Presbyterian committee used a telephone interviewing process to talk with 225 persons who had been removed from the membership rolls of local congregations and a like number of active Presbyterians. The committee found that the dropouts were less likely than the active members to describe their church as being friendly, warm, and personally satisfying.[48]

Schaller has reported that there is evidence which indicates that one-third and even as many as one-half of the members of all Protestant churches do not feel that they belong or fit into the congregation of which they are members.[49] Schaller elsewhere has indicated that slightly less than one-third of all inactive members were unhappy about the congregation of which they were now former members. A very frequent complaint of these people was that they did not feel they were accepted by longtime members of the congregation or by individuals who served as its leaders.[50]

Certain types of people are particularly likely to feel unaccepted. Examples of such types include "the person who marries a member, but does not feel accepted in his or her own right . . . single young adults . . . childless couples who join what turns out to be a very child-centered parish . . . the person from a nationality background different from that of most of the members . . . the new member who never becomes comfortable with the order of worship or music of this congregation."[51]

Schaller has also asserted that people become inactive because they are unable to find a group in the congregation of which to be a part. This statement implicitly affirms the importance of positive relationships as motivators of active participation in the life of a congregation.[52] Perhaps individuals who grew up in small rural congregations which were made up of a limited number of extended families and who migrate to the city and join large urban or suburban congregations might be representative of a type of person who would drop out because of not being able to find a group in which to participate.

Rauff has reported that inactive Roman Catholic lay persons say that an impersonal quality was characteristic of their former parish churches. Rauff concludes that people are not willing to accept alienation and impersonality in their parishes.[53]

Of course, the data collected by Savage, which was reported earlier, also affirms how conflicts with clergy, family members, and fellow church members can be the precipitating event which causes people to withdraw from the life of a parish.

The importance of relationships for motivating individuals to join a congregation and the maintenance of those relationships for continued participation in the life of a congregation may be well established sociologically and psychologically, but these factors are difficult for many to accept. Perhaps pastors particularly want to believe that the primary motivation for initial and continued affiliation is commitment to the Gospel of Jesus Christ. For some, emphasis on relationships may appear to cheapen the integrity of church membership or call into question the quality of members' personal relationship with Christ.

This factor has caused Dudley to write: "Implicit in membership withdrawal is a curious double standard. When people unite with a congregation, they resist suggesting personal needs or social satisfactions as causes for joining. They consciously relate church membership with program participation and religious values. When they leave, however, they are more likely to blame a breakdown in personal relationships."[54]

But perhaps even more frightening to many parish leaders is the fact that if relationships are so important then repair of broken relationships must become a high priority concern of clerical and lay leaders. Most congregational leaders do not have the skills, temperament, and patience to serve effectively as facilitators to repair relationships. Theologically, leaders have to come to grips with the nature of anger; psychologically, they have to learn how to dissipate anger; and methodologically, they must be skilled at resolving the underlying conflict that produced the angry reactions in the first place. More will be said later about how parish leaders can work through anger and assist in restoring relationships.

Dropouts have relatively strong negative attitudes toward sermons. Greeley has indicated that the quality of sermons is an important issue when considering Roman Catholic involvement in church. Greeley judges that the quality of sermons is a more important variable than "clericalism, feminism, racism, and in some respects even more important than sexual attitudes."[55] In this same source Greeley writes, "People like their parishes if sermons are good."[56] Rauff also found that inactive Roman Catholic people said that the sermons they had heard in church were not very stirring.[57] Enslin portrays the situation in broad strokes when he says: "I believe that many folk today who are quite content to loll in bed of a Sunday morning or to fill the hours with the leafing of a Sunday paper, would be willing, even eager, to go to a church where they would truly feel at home and where they might find fresh strength and insight for the problems they face and the tasks they must meet. In a word, let the preaching be directed to men of the present day and be couched in a style which is understandable and worth listening to, and pews will gradually fill up again. Preaching has not become outdated. It has simply become deadly dull."[58]

Many people recognize that pastors are very instrumental in setting the tone for the life of the parish. According to Schaller, less than a quarter of inactive members cite unhappiness with their pastor's ministry as a primary consideration for their inactivity.[59] When people do indicate their unhappiness with the ministry of their pastor, numerous facets of the unhappiness are identified. Some people join a church when a specific pastor is leading it. When he moves on to a new assignment, resigns, or retires, they become dropouts. Other people mention that they had theological differences with the pastor or that the pastor did not serve their needs adequately in a time of crisis. Other people indicate that the pastor or priest is insensitive, not the right age, incapable of dealing with conflict in a creative manner, and incompatible with them in personality and style. Still others say that they have had specific experiences with the pastor which have created anxiety or that they disagree with the pastor concerning how to prioritize meeting the needs of the parish.[60] Among Roman Catholics, priests are valued if they lead their parishes with a democratic style and value and maintain a busy, active parish life.[61] Inactive Roman Catholics are often critical of the fact that parish priests do not know their parishioners. The size of many Roman Catholic churches makes it almost impossible for the priests to know their people. But this lack of personal contact is seen by some inactives as the reason why people drop out initially and do not return subsequently to active parish participation.[62]

These responses seem to confirm Womack's contention that a congregation cannot grow any larger than it has the ability to care for a specific number of people. He contends that there is a direct relationship between a church's base of operational efficiency and effectiveness and its membership size.[63]

In interviewing 225 inactive Presbyterians and a like number of active Presbyterians, a United Presbyterian committee found that the inactive former members were less likely to describe their former pastor as "effective and inspiring."[64]

These data indicate that how positively people respond to the pastor of a congregation is important, but it is not the most important variable when considering why people have become inactive.

Because of the widespread publicity that surrounded theological conflicts in a number of denominations, many people assume that differences over doctrine are the cause of many people dropping out of local churches. Schaller has written that only a small percentage of inactives have become inactive because they disagree with their denominations.[65] A study of 225 inactive Presbyterians determined that these inactives knew Presbyterian doctrine well, but they disagreed with the content of the doctrine more frequently than had respondents from a control group of 225 active Presbyterians.[66] The findings of the studies reviewed by Dudley caused him to conclude that, "Generally, membership dropouts were far more apt to leave in boredom than in disagreement" over theological matters.[67]

Studies in religious sociology done during the 1950s and 1960s seemed to suggest that doctrinal matters were very important variables. For whatever reasons (i.e., less concern about doctrine, more discriminating questions by data gatherers, more sophisticated research models and designs, etc.) doctrinal concerns seem to be a less important variable in determining peoples' actions relative to involvement in churches today.

Metz discovered that after spouse and family considerations the next most important reason for inactivity was that the inactive people had given over more of their time to such pursuits as camping, boating, and involvement in other organizations. Perhaps if Metz could have analyzed the individuals' process of dropping out he would have discovered that these activities were less the cause than the result of their dropping out. All that can be said for sure is that people who are not active in church will probably be more involved in leisure-time activities.[68]

William McKinney has used the term "the otherwise engaged" to describe people who are involved in "more interesting or compelling activities."[69]

There is some evidence to suggest that the unchurched are people who do not participate in other "community-building enterprises, associations, and institutions in our society."[70] In fact, at least two studies showed that three-fourths of the unchurched said that they did not participate in any voluntary organization. At this stage of the art it is impossible to state with any certainty how this observation fits into the mosaic of church dropouts. However, it seems safe to suggest that there may well be a significant percentage of people among the church dropouts who are alienated from society and who might be described as living on its margins.[71]

The 225 nonactive Presbyterians interviewed by the United Presbyterian committee were more likely to say that "an individual should arrive at his own religious beliefs quite independent of the church" than were the control group of active Presbyterians.[72]

These data agree with data from other studies which demonstrate that a great number of American citizens feel that they can have and express the Christian faith without benefit of the church. Numerous public opinion polls have established that many people claim Christianity as their faith even though they do not attend or belong to a Christian congregation.[73] Thus individualism as a commitment seems to encourage at least some Christian people to abstain from joining a church initially or to become dropouts.

Another aspect of this riddle is the observation of Womack, who says that Americans who do not participate in the life of the church are inactive not because they have some major differences of opinion with Christianity but because they are nonattenders by habit.[74]

Some inactive members reflect a lack of denominational loyalty. The reasons for this are multifaceted. Probable causes include factors like moving too much, unhappiness with a given congregation in the denomination, disdain for the doctrine of the denomination, poor religious training, confrontation with a clergyman of the denomination, etc.[75]

Particularly in some of the more conservative denominations common sense suggests to congregational leaders that a congregation's involvement in social action activities will cause more people to become inactive than if a congregation does not involve itself in such projects. However, the 1978 Gallup poll found that 30 percent of all nonaffiliated persons and 32 percent of people who were church-related agreed with the survey statement: "Most churches and synagogues today are not concerned enough with social justice."[76] In addition the poll results seem to show that on a national basis more people drop out of the church because the church is not active enough in the social arena than drop out because the church is too active in causes for social justice.[77]

Other studies have shown that growing congregations are more likely to be involved in social action pursuits[78] than declining congregations. In light of these new data about the relationship of social action and congregational dynamics, Dudley has written: "Growing churches are involved; declining churches fight about involvement" in social action.[79]

Individuals who have become inactive sometimes explain their behavior in relationship to another person's behavior. This process is called scapegoating. It is a kind of rationalization process. It is a way people use to escape taking responsibility for their actions. Such scapegoating is also used as a means of self-justification. The actions of others "prove" the correctness of their own behavior in comparison to the hypocritical actions of those who attend church regularly.[80]

Schaller has reported that more than one-third of inactive Protestants became inactive because when they moved away from the community in which their church was located they did not bother to ask for a letter of transfer. This particular statistic is somber, for it implies lack of a soul-caring mentality on the part of the previous congregation and pastor.

The method used to affiliate with a congregation initially is also significant. If people join a congregation by baptism as infants or by junior confirmation, they are more likely to drop out than individuals who join by letters of transfer.[81]

There are four stages in the life cycle which seem to make it more likely that people will become dropouts. These have been highlighted earlier, but they are so important that they need to be repeated. People are more likely to drop out of church during the first two years they live in a new community, when they are between 15 and 23 years old, during the first few years after their youngest child has moved away from home, and just after they are divorced.[82]

Even more general reasons for becoming inactive are factors like advanced age, illness, specific physical limitations, the loss of a spouse in death, and inability to find transportation to church.[83]

The findings of the studies cited in this chapter should be viewed as being representative and not exhaustive. However, these findings do reflect the great diversity of concerns and motivations which seem to cause people to withdraw from the life of a local congregation. This great diversity of concerns and motivations gives credance to the claims made in the initial paragraph of this chapter. To address the issue of dropping out one must be willing to assume that the problem and its solution are complex. Simplistic problem identification and simple solutions at the congregational level will probably result in disillusionment and cynicism on the part of active members and heightened anger and resentments among those who have become inactive.

# Chapter 2

# Preventive Measures to Limit the Number of Dropouts

The previous chapter described inactive persons and identified the primary motivations they cite for becoming inactive. Trying to design measures to prevent members from dropping out and attempting to make necessary changes to meet the concerns of inactives is surrounded by a number of questions.

The two most important questions are: "What motivates Christians to be concerned about individuals who become inactive?" and "Are some types of methodology employed to maintain membership not suitable for Christian people?" The previous chapter could persuade people to become very mechanistic and manipulative towards the inactives. Therefore, at the outset of this chapter, it is necessary to affirm that the church on earth is Christ's body. It is Christ who is the Head of that body. Christ sets the agenda for the individual and corporate members of His body. It would be most unfortunate if the findings of all our empirical studies gave us the feeling that we can manage the crisis of loss or potential loss of faith if we only do the "right things." Such thoughts are the thoughts of sinful human beings who wish to supplant Christ as the Head of His body.

The language St. Paul uses in First Corinthians emphasizes that Christ's body is an organism and not an organization.[1] Since in its theological nature the church is not an organization as it is in its sociological nature, in spiritual matters it cannot be controlled by human managers in the way that General Motors or American Telephone and Telegraph are controlled by human managers.[2]

Yet as mainline denominations have approached the problem of membership decline they have tended to follow a managerial approach. Implicit in this approach is the assumption that the fortunes of the church can be controlled by human beings. There is an underlying hypothesis here which calls into question the basic theological proposition that the church is God's church and that He is finally in control of its well-being.[3]

Having indicated the central issue, it is imperative that Christ's people recognize that an important question that needs to be asked of the leadership of every congregation is, "What are we intentionally doing to minimize the number of people who drop out of our congregation each year?" While it is well and good to answer, "We have services every Sunday, the sacraments are administered, Bible classes and Sunday school classes are taught," etc., these activities may or may not be effective in retaining membership. It is imperative that every congregation have as one of its explicitly stated goals the retention of members, along with specific strategies which help accomplish that goal.

Theologically, the reason for concern to prevent dropouts has nothing to do with meeting local and national budgets or comparisons of denominations or congregations. Retention of members is a concern because Christian people care about the spiritual well-being of fellow members.

## Christian Concern About Inactivity

Theologically, the issue of retention revolves around the conviction that in the life of the local church the spiritual needs of people can be met only when the Word and sacraments are used by members. These means of grace are the conduits through which God communicates His wonderful plan of salvation. It is through these means of grace that individual Christians are initially called together and subsequently maintained in the corporate life of local congregations.

The motive for being concerned about the church attendance of members is that provided by the writer of the Letter to the Hebrews, where in verse 25 of chapter 10 he exhorts his readers not to neglect to meet together in worship. Often, when this passage is applied, dire warnings are offered about the fact that absenting oneself from the assemblies of God's people places one in spiritual jeopardy. This application of the text is certainly warranted when the verses which follow it are also considered. To become apostate means that a person has spurned the Son of God and has outraged the Holy Spirit (Heb. 10:29). Such a person will experience the vengeance of God (Heb. 10:30-31).

This concern is reflected in the often-used story told about the great evangelist Dwight L. Moody. As this story has it, Moody was asked by some person why it was necessary for Christian people to go to church. Moody did not answer the question. He merely went to the fireplace, took a red-hot coal out of the fire and placed it on the hearth, and left the room. When he returned later, the coal was no longer burning. Separated from the other burning material, the coal had gone out. The person is alleged to have said to Dr. Moody that he now realized the answer to his question. Moody had offered him a very sobering truth without saying a word.

But this passage from Hebrews also has another emphasis that is less often perceived when the passage is explained or applied. In a number of places in the New Testament, particularly First Corinthians 12, St. Paul argues that spiritual gifts are offered to the total church through the gifts that God gives to its individual members. Not only do persons short-change themselves and make themselves vulnerable to apostasy when they forsake the assembly of God's people, they also shortchange the other members of the local congregation. Christian people have been given both the right and the privilege of stirring up one another to love and good works. Christian people can provide meaningful encourage-ment to one another. The spiritual gifts that have been given to them are for the edification of others. When they withdraw from the fellowship, their gifts are no longer available to their fellow Christians.

Thus there are at least two major theological reasons why church leaders are concerned about people dropping out of church. The first is the realization that people are incapable of edifying themselves. The second is that withdrawal means that people have a self-centered piety which fails to take seriously how important their gifts are for the well-being of the entire fellowship.

Numerous Christian writers have reminded their readers that the characteristic of Christians which impressed observers in the first century A.D. was the fact that Christian people loved one another. That love was impressive because it went beyond feelings to demonstrations of caring, sharing, and doing for one another.[4] Such loving, caring, sharing, and doing includes being eager to take steps to prevent the cooling and/or dying of another Christian's faith.

## Retention Through Careful Initial Assimilation

In recent years social scientists have helped church leaders appreciate the importance of assimilating new members into the congregation. In many communities a congregation cannot assume that the assimilating forces present in ethnic, rural parishes are also present in its community. In ethnic, rural congregations or ethnic congregations in stable metropolitan neighborhoods, family ties and close community relationships provide the means for individuals to become assimilated to parish life. Baptisms, first Communions, confirmations, weddings, wedding anniversaries, and funerals—and the parties or gatherings which accompany these events—help to assimilate individuals into the congregation and assist people in retaining active membership. In highly mobile, metropolitan congregations individual nuclear families are cut off from such assimilating forces.

Therefore preventive maintenance programs must include means of assimilating new members into the congregation and including new members in some meaningful support groups(s). Most members can be retained only if they can be helped to be more than members in name alone. Planned approaches to assimilate new members into the mission and ministry of the congregation are critical if the congregation is going to be serious about retaining members. Without assimilation the congregation will find that its open doors only lead to backdoors through which new members quickly exit.[5]

## Retention Through Emphasis on Positive Forces

Just as there are types of people and specific motivations that seem to encourage members to drop out of congregational life, there are also types of people and specific motivations that help members to remain active. A realistic preventive maintenance program at the parish level needs to maximize the holding power of these elements while at the same time realizing that such maximization may cause alienation among those who do not fit the categories. The needs of these latter people for inclusion may be met by using other methods, which will be presented later.

A family tradition of membership in the same congregation is a solidifying force. When second and third generations of the same family are members of a specific congregation, there will be less likelihood of withdrawing. Individuals who stay fixed in one place long enough so that second and third generations can be members of a given parish may well be in the minority of the total U. S. population. Yet the solidarity of many small rural parishes depends heavily on this motivator.[6]

When families do move from one geographical location to another, if they join a congregation of the same denomination they are less likely to become dropouts than if they were to join a congregation of a different denomination.[7] Considerations such as denominational loyalty, the likelihood of homogeneity within the denominational group, familiarity with worship patterns and hymnody, having similar expectations as other members concerning what constitutes a good sermon and positive parish life *may* all be components of the social, psychological, and theological glue that helps such individuals remain active.

Denominational loyalty seems to make it possible for people to "weather" certain storms in their personal or congregational lives which would cause the average person to stop participating in the life of a congregation. This denominational loyalty may be created by attending a school[8] or college supported by the denomination, or by having relatives who are loyal clergy serving in the denomination's ministerium and on national or local boards or committees of the denomination and its auxiliaries.[9]

There are a number of ways that the retaining power of denominational loyalty can be helpfully employed. Many people drop out of church life because as they move from place to place they do not take the time necessary to transfer membership to congregations in their new communities. The transfer of membership can be facilitated if the congregational leaders of the former parish: (1) inform the persons or families concerning the names and addresses of congregations located in the vicinity of their new residence, (2) communicate with the leadership of these congregations and advise those leaders of the names and addresses of the persons taking up residence in their area, and (3) communicate with the families once they have moved and encourage them to visit a church in their new community. In turn, the congregations in the new community must follow through on these leads.

Follow-up activities on the part of both the former and new congregations are time-consuming. Yet a program of responsible soul care makes this operation absolutely necessary. No other program designed thus far by denominations (based upon changes of address for national church publications, etc.) is as effective as the care that can be manifested by local congregations. Personal letters sent by congregational leaders to former members two or three weeks after they have moved (with carbons sent to the pastors in the new areas), encouraging them to visit the new local churches, and personal letters to the new pastors asking them to call on the persons (with carbons to the former members) are powerful tools to motivate the former members to activity and the leadership of the area congregations to responsible action.

The need for quick action in regard to individuals who move to a new location is substantiated by the findings of Walrath. If congregations in the community to which people move do not relate quickly to the newcomers, the newcomers will feel isolated and will conclude that the congregations truly accept only natives of the community. Walrath found that newcomers will relate to the churches in their new community very soon after they relocate. If the congregations give the impression that their ministries are only designed for natives, newcomers will tend not to join such congregations.

A second opportunity may arise for the newcomers to move toward one of these congregations if sometime later the newcomers need help in working through a crisis. If the crisis comes long enough after the move and the newcomers have been able to develop other support groups, the newcomers may not need the ministry of a congregation even in times of crisis.[10]

Another aspect of using denominational loyalty for membership retention is the need to continue establishing new congregations. Perhaps the vast majority of congregations in the United States have begun as Presbyterian, Methodist, Baptist, Lutheran, etc. Christians have asked their national bodies through local judicatories to start new congregations to meet their spiritual needs. In a time of ecumenical activity which discourages competition and an era of shortages of building funds coupled with high land and building costs that make church planting, as we have come to know it, difficult at best and impossible at worst, almost all mainline denominations have cut back on the number of new parishes that have been started. These cutbacks have negatively affected church growth and have strained the denominational loyalties of certain people as they have moved into areas where their former denominations are not represented at all or are underrepresented.[11]

## Retention Through Improved Worship Experiences

Worship is the expression of the spiritual life of a congregation and is the focus of much feeling and commitment on the part of members.[12]

Congregational leaders and clergy can do something about the worship practices of the congregation. Since uninspiring worship is often cited as a reason for dropping out of church, worship issues are important to consider. Worship properly understood is comprised of those actions which God's people do for God. In worship, people are the actors, and God is the audience. Worship celebrates the goodness of a loving God. Worship ought not be something which we "grind out" week after week. Worship ought to be fun, exciting, exhilarating, and positive. Liturgical worship can possess these qualities if the worship leader understands the nature of worship and avoids the rut of deadening routine.[13]

Stott has written: "We need worship services that express the reality of the living God and joyfully celebrate Jesus Christ's victory over sin and death. Too often routine supplants reality, and the liturgy (if any) becomes lugubrious. I think public worship should always be dignified, but it is unforgivable to make it dull."[14]

How a congregation feels about worship seems to be an indication of its internal climate. Congregations that are growing, and have a positive self-concept, have positive feelings about worship. However, in declining churches the subject of worship produces controversy.[15]

As leaders of congregations try to stem the tide of backdoor loses, the evaluation of worship services within those congregations is a matter of importance. It is imperative that the reactions of members concerning worship be solicited, studied, and evaluated, and that necessary and constructive changes be made. At the same time, leaders should note the caution that if their congregation is declining in membership much more is probably at stake than how the worship services are being conducted. In such cases, conflict management skills may be even more important than making changes in worship patterns and practices.

## Retention Through Improved Preaching

Since many dropouts are critical of the preaching they heard in their former parish, the improvement of preaching is an important concern.

This is a multifaceted issue. Members tend to respond more positively to preaching if it comes from clergy who are judged to have genuine love and concern for the members of the parish. Such love and concern are manifested when the pastor knows everyone by name, is willing to minister to people in every condition of life, and lives his life in congruity with what he preaches.

From a Lutheran vantage point, good sermons must set forth Law and Gospel properly distinguished from one another and must give the Gospel predominate emphasis. Dr. Robert Kolb's book, *The Theology for Evangelism*, in this series gives expression to this emphasis in very helpful ways.

Preaching does not exist in a vacuum. Good preachers are able to relate the faith to the realities of life at the particular point in history where they are. For example, the 1970s have been called the "Me Decade." All kinds of popular self-help psychologies attempted to confront the guilt that people naturally feel as sinful people. But no amount of rationalizing or exclaiming that people are inherently okay will meet their spiritual needs. Finally it is only the forgiveness that God makes available in the death and resurrection of Christ that empowers, strengthens, and affirms His people.

Sermons need to convey in a helpful manner God's wonderful plan of freeing people from feelings of guilt and insecurity and must provide realistic suggestions concerning how God's people might respond to God's good news. Preachers need to help their listeners see Jesus as the only Savior of mankind. Then, as a logical outgrowth of hearing and appropriating the good news, preachers need to assist Christian people in perceiving how their lives might be lived in service to the God who has granted them salvation.

Stott has observed: "Evangelical preaching tends to be biblical but not contemporary, liberal preaching contemporary but not biblical. Why must we polarize? It is the combination of the two that is so powerful. It is a rare phenomenon."[16] It is Biblical-contemporary preaching which helps maintain the commitment of people to the church, because such preaching applies the power of the Gospel effectively to the conditions in which people find themselves day in and day out.

## Retention Through Effective Pastoral Care

The ministry style of pastors is an important issue for causing a limited percentage of people to become inactive. Denominational leaders and bishops who have the major responsibility for assisting congregations in making decisions about calling or contracting of pastoral leadership are often only intuitively aware of concerns that need to be addressed.

Generally speaking, pastors are likely to be most effective when they are able to serve in congregations and live in communities which most closely parallel their abilities, interests, perceptions, and values.[17] During the late '60s and early '70s much was written about the need for pastors to play the prophetic role rather than the shepherding role in congregations. If one's assumption is that effective pastors have the responsibility to make the comfortable uncomfortable and the uncomfortable comfortable, then the general principle stated above may need to be modified a bit.

Second, pastors are more likely to be effective if they attempt to meet the needs of their members and of their community. "Meeting the needs of people" and "working with people where they are" are cliches in the helping professions.[18] Yet all too frequently pastors arrive on the scene with their programs, which they get their new congregation to adopt during the honeymoon period, and then they find that the adopted programs do not produce the expected results. Pastors conclude that the people are not really committed, for if they were committed they would be much more responsive and the newly adopted programs would be more productive. What pastors fail to realize is that the congregation was made up of people before the pastor arrived and many of those same people will still be members of the congregation after the pastor leaves to take on new responsibilities. In the same way, those members will remain in the community long after the pastor has departed. Therefore the parishioners have a sense of history and of the future which serves as an internal gyroscope and causes them to recognize almost intuitively what approaches will or will not be effective.

It is no small task for subjective people to be objective. Pastors also suffer the burden of subjectivity. There is a fine line between arrogant subjectivity and critical insight. Pastors who are unable to distinguish between legitimate caution and a foot-dragging obstinance will cause themselves and their people much needless pain.

Third, some pastors have a special propensity for attracting people with spiritual and emotional problems. Often these problem-riddled people are highly dependent on the caring ministry of their pastor. One liability of this pastoral emphasis is that these problem-plagued people will not be able to assume leadership roles in the congregation. There is obviously a need for ministry to troubled people. Christ's own ministry demonstrated that truth clearly. However, the liability of such a ministry is that other commonly expected aspects of ministry can be undercut and ignored, which causes the less-troubled members to feel dissatisfied. A second liability is that when such a pastor resigns or leaves to take on other charges the problem-plagued people often become dropouts. Their membership in the congregation is dependent on their relationship to the pastor involved. The crucial message here seems to be that pastors should make a caring ministry possible, yet not be dominated by the need to do the majority of that caring ministry themselves.

In the fourth place, there are pastors who demand to be involved in everything that happens in the congregation. Their personality, or their concept of ministry, or their need to dominate, or whatever, causes them to become indispensable for everything that transpires in the congregation. Where such pastoral leadership is provided, the membership of the congregation does not get organized enough, is not experienced enough, and becomes passive enough so that, when the pastor leaves the congregation, the congregation falls apart.[19] People from these congregations appear among the statistics of those who became inactive when their pastor left the congregation. Such congregations also tend not to develop social cohesiveness between their members. Therefore, because such congregations lack organization and social cohesiveness, there is a much greater likelihood that members will become inactive during pastoral vacancies or when less dominant pastors begin to employ their own styles of ministry.

Finally, pastors who found new congregations and who maintain control over them will discover that such a congregation will grow only as large as the number of members the pastor is able to serve effectively.[20] Thus, if a given pastor can only effectively serve 250 members, the congregation will remain at 250 members. As new ones are gained, older ones drop out. The congregation's system and the ministry style of the pastor can accommodate only 250 members.

Much more could be written about how styles of pastoral ministry can affect the dropout rate. We hope enough examples have been included to highlight the nature of the question.

Conscientious pastors need to reflect on their styles of ministry to try to determine how their approaches to ministry may be contributing to the number of people who are becoming inactive. Such reflection should not be done to produce guilt. Perhaps such reflection should not even be done for the purpose of changing styles of ministry, although changes may be appropriate in some situations. But such reflection should be done in order to evaluate whether pastor and congregation are suitably matched in personal attributes and commitments. Since human beings are notoriously subjective, an "objective" outside consultant or an "objective" evaluation instrument may be of assistance in collecting and evaluating germane data.

## Retention Through Christian Education

Many social scientists and denominational statisticians have noted that in the mainline denominations of the United States the number of infant baptisms declined during the late 1950s and 1960s. What caused this significant decline in numbers is still under study. During this period there was an even greater percentage of decline in church school enrollments. The church school enrollment is a very reliable predictor of what church membership will be in five to ten years.[21]

An analysis of the data reported in the 1980 *Statistical Yearbook of The Lutheran Church—Missouri Synod* demonstrates the nature of the problem. There were 72,756 babies baptized in LCMS congregations in 1966. Of this group of babies, 51,092 or 70 percent were enrolled in Sunday school when they were three years old. Then 40,926 or 56 percent of these babies were confirmed at the completion of their confirmation instruction, normally done at age 14. Finally, 13,092 or 17 percent of these 1966 babies participated in Sunday morning Bible classes after confirmation.[22]

These data agree with the data produced by national surveys conducted over the years which have demonstrated that there has been a decline in the percentage of the American population who have received some religious education during childhood. Between 1952 and 1965 the decline was slight. But between 1965 and 1978 the decline was precipitous.[23]

Another important bit of information which is impossible to collect, but which would be interesting to know, is the number of 1966 babies born to LCMS members who were never baptized and so were never reflected in the numbers presented above.

These data suggest areas of intervention by the leaders of local congregations. Systematic follow-up is needed to ensure that all babies born to members of the congregation are baptized. Once these babies are baptized, concerted efforts need to be expended to encourage parents to enroll the children in Sunday school. Careful instruction and care of the children by Sunday school teachers and professional ministers of the congregation should enable the congregation to confirm a high percentage of these children at age 14. A positive, energetic, program of youth ministry, capable of encouraging spiritual maturity, is essential to retain the children who have been confirmed.

Obviously, the retention of young members through programs of soul care and Christian education is very important. The Southern Baptist Convention has centered much attention on the Sunday school. A study done by the Methodist Church suggests that perhaps as many as 70 to 80 percent of its new members are children of church families.[24] Sometimes church growth authors call this retention process "biological growth." Whatever the name used, it is clear that efforts must be applied to children in order to retain them.

The above comments, although well meaning, are perhaps too simplistic because the major contributors to childhood religious experience have less to do with congregational programming for children than with the powerful influence that parents have on their children's religious training. The religious influence that parents have on children depends on the faith of husband and wife, the building block upon which the nuclear family's faith commitment depends.

The data reported in Chapter 1 demonstrated the importance of a spouse's effect on the other spouse's religious response. This insight does not need to strike terror in the hearts of the leaders of congregations or cause them to feel that the task before them is hopeless.

In his study of lapsed church members Rauff found that, particularly among Roman Catholics, participation in Marriage Encounter events had helped to bring adults back to the church. To a lesser degree Rauff learned that Marriage Encounter also had similar effects on people who had dropped out of other denominations. Most of the people indicated that they had given up on the church prior to the weekend when they experienced the Marriage Encounter. However, the profound impact of the Encounter experience caused them to take another look at the church. The Encounter experience had caused them to recognize that the church had something to say about a very important, personal aspect of their lives.[25]

The marriage enrichment movement in its many manifestations throughout the United States does more than make a contribution to the happiness of various couples. Marriage enrichment programming in the context of local congregations attests to the fact that the church has something to say to the most fundamental building block of all society and of congregations, namely the family unit revolving around a devout husband and wife who take their commitment to God and to one another very seriously.

## Retention Through Ministry to Young Adults

Congregations that are serious about stemming the tide of backdoor losses must address the staggering losses that particularly mainline denominations have experienced from among young adult members. Dudley has asserted that the absence of young people "is the cause of declining church membership."[26] Numerous studies[27] have documented the fact that young adults who have attended college are very likely to possess values and wish to live life-styles that are very different from those of older adult members of mainline congregations. In fact, during the late '60s and '70s every survey taken by sociologists of religion suggested that the gap between the values and attitudes of young adults and older adults grew with the passage of each year.[28]

These data imply that those congregations and denominations whose memberships do not contain many college-educated young adults have not suffered the same kind of defections among the young as did those congregations and denominations who had a much higher percentage of their membership attending and graduating from college.[29]

These data also suggest that mainline denominations will continue to experience difficulties retaining their college-educated young adults as active members in their congregations. Dudley states that "these young people represent the lost members of mainline churches."[30]

There are at least two major proposals concerning how congregations might wish to prevent the exodus of so many of their young members. One major proposal is that congregations should become willing to be more open to diversity within their midst and grant to young people the option to pursue the values and commitments they and their age group have adopted. In the words of Niebuhr, this option is almost "The Christ of Culture"[31] approach. Christ and culture are judged to be synonymous. This call to permit diversity is certainly problematic. From the vantage point of this author, some of the values being espoused by many younger adults—such as the permissibility of premarital and extramarital sexual relationships and abortion on demand—are clearly not Biblically acceptable.

The other major approach moves across the spectrum. It is the position of "Christ the Transformer of Culture."[32] In this approach the advice given to congregations and denominations is that a youth culture which has evil and godless values and commitments must be exposed as such. Hutchenson argues that such a message is not only the proper one to convey; it is also the message that works. In support of this contention he cites the successes of nondenominational evangelical youth organizations.[33] Included in this approach is the emphasis on enrolling elementary and secondary students in Christian schools and encouraging college students to attend evangelical colleges.[34]

Clearly these two approaches stand in stark contrast to one another. In many ways each proposal allows the leaders of congregations and denominations to give expression to their theological and ideological commitments and assumptions. The march of history suggests that neither ideological extreme is the panacea. Each position has strengths and weaknesses. Yet since the most recent experience of mainline denominations has tended toward the liberal end of the spectrum, it is not surprising that the call is now going out to move toward a more conservative position.

Only the passage of time will determine if the actions taken now and in the near future will be corrective or if they will be reactive and produce a climate in which other abuses will be accented and new problems created. The issue of retaining young people as members of mainline denominations is complex and will not be addressed adequately with simplistic actions and programs.

## Retention Through Positive Interpersonal Relationships

Since social dislocations are a part of modern urban life, there is an ongoing need for members of congregations to satisfy their yearning for close interpersonal relationships.[35] In the late 1950s, '60s, and into the '70s many books on the subject of congregational renewal tended to poke fun at or even lambaste all the "fellowship" activities going on in congregations. One pundit suggested that in some future age when archaeologists would excavate our churches they would conclude that cooking was part of the Christian religion because of all the elaborate kitchens they would find in churches. Spaghetti suppers, potlucks, and a whole host of other activities were lampooned because they were judged quasi-religious activities. Many pastors tried to redirect women's guild programs, men's clubs, fellowship clubs, couples' clubs, etc., into more specifically religious activities like Bible studies and prayer groups. Hindsight suggests that these changes may have eroded the social, psychological, and theological glue that helps people remain active in congregations.

Participation in Bible study or prayer groups encourages church members to remain active.[36] From the vantage point of Lutheran theology one would expect that if members are recipients of the means of grace, Word and Sacrament, then such people would experience the active power of the Holy Spirit in their lives. Active involvement in worship and continued reception of the means of grace are aspects of the sanctified life. From the vantage point of social science theories one would expect such individuals to remain active because the group in which they participate has become integral in their understanding of themselves. Because of the discoveries about how small groups can contribute to the overall strength of the large group, the importance of groups for maintaining church members' sense of well-being and identification in the congregation has been highlighted in recent years. The Church Growth Movement has been especially vocal in its support of small groups within the life of the local church.

However, there are groups and there are groups. Small groups are most beneficial when their leaders understand the purpose of the group activity and how best to fulfill that purpose. Group theory offers helpful insights here. Depending on which theorist one reads, one gets varying descriptions; but most theorists have agreed that after considering the purpose of any given group there are basically four major types of leadership styles that are appropriate for group leaders. These leadership styles have been named: (1) High Relationship and Low Task, (2) High Task and High Relationship, (3) Low Task and Low Relationship, and (4) High Task and Low Relationship.[37]

The high relationship and low task style may be very appropriate for a couples' club in the local congregation. It emphasizes the relationships between people. However, a task-oriented person who wants to do more than relate with other members may feel frustrated and complain that "nothing ever gets done" by the couples' club. If he persists in trying to get the couples' club to do something, like a mission project, he will alienate himself from the members whose basic needs for a group emphasizing high relationship and low task are being met with the club's original programming.

Groups that can be described as high task and low relationship depend on a very directive leadership style. This approach works best with a group that is in the process of development or one that does not know what its purpose is. But it is not helpful in mature groups where the group's sense of purpose is accepted by all.

Newer groups need leadership which emphasizes high task and high relationship goals. This leadership style becomes inappropriate when the members have taken responsibility both for the health of the group and for the tasks it has set out to do.

Mature groups who are meeting relationship needs and fulfilling group tasks are best led with a low task and low relationship style of leadership. But new groups would find this style frustrating, weak, and ineffective.

All the above factors illustrate that while active groups in a congregation can be positive and helpful in maintaining allegiance, groups which are improperly led or organized can actually be a liability and produce feelings of conflict and hostility which contribute to individuals becoming apathetic or bored and finally inactive.

Certain skills help people to function in group settings. Verbal skills are very important in many aspects of life, including participation in groups. It is not surprising, then, that people with well developed verbal skills are less likely to be church dropouts than those who have less-than-average verbal abilities.[38]

## Retention Through Significant Experiences and Personal Investment

Individuals who have had a significant experience happen to them while they are members of a congregation are less likely to withdraw from that congregation than those members who have not had such a significant experience. Baptism, confirmation, marriage, and the funeral of a relative or a close friend are examples of such significant experiences.[39]

When people have made a sizable positive investment in a congregation, they are less likely to withdraw. They have "earned" their place in the parish because of their activities.[40] Dudley suggests an annual homecoming event for small congregations. Such events have some value for former members and older members of the congregation, but the primary value is that new members are included in the planning and carrying out of the event. This helps the new members to identify with the congregation, assists older members in accepting the new members, and makes retention of the new members much more likely.[41]

Another way of helping old and new members of a congregation accept one another has to do with how new members are helped to appropriate the unique history of a congregation. New members can be "brought on board" through older members' telling of the congregation's informal history. This storytelling may be facilitated if it is done informally after a meal, using slides and photographs along with short, interesting anecdotes told by some older members of the congregation.[42]

Because congregations are large enough and enduring enough, they become highly institutionalized when compared to some ad hoc groups that form to meet a particular short-term need and then disband. Because of the pressures to institutionalize, leaders of congregations often forget that God did not put people on earth to make them fodder for institutions; rather institutions are formed by people in order to serve people. When the proper understanding of the nature of institutions is lost, the members of such institutions feel they have become means to the end of institutional development, and they feel a sense of conflict between themselves and other members of the institutions and with the institutions themselves.[43] Members who are distraught by the conflict they have experienced and members who feel used often drop out of congregational life.

## Retention Through Conflict Resolution

Chapter 1 placed emphasis on the important role unresolved conflicts in interpersonal relationships play in causing people to withdraw from congregations. Because conflict destroys congregations, leaders of congregations need to possess conflict-resolution skills.

In an article entitled "Seminarians Unprepared for Parish 'Give and Take,'" the author wrote: "Managing, inspiring team work, and resolving conflicts are not course titles at most seminaries, but they should be, according to a study conducted by The Alban Institute. . . . The scholarship and theory of seminary training does not prepare pastors for the 'frequent and unexpected responsibility for resolving conflicts,' said project director Roy M. Oswald. . . ."[44]

An important assumption of theorists in the field of conflict

44

resolution is that conflict is an inevitable factor in all situations where two or more people must interact with one another. Therefore the issue is not whether there will be conflict. The issue is, "How shall the conflict be managed?"

There are a number of possibilities that may help to explain why church leaders and members are so inept in working through conflicts. Perhaps church leaders and members expect that among Christian people there should be no conflict. Since the love of Christ motivates His people, some faithful people seemingly conclude that conflict should not exist within congregations. Such reasoning is not founded on Scripture, for it relates examples of conflict between faithful disciples. Scripture gives us an excellent example of wise conflict resolution in Acts 15. James wisely resolved the conflict between Jewish and Gentile believers by appealing to the authoritative Scriptures, which were accepted by both factions.

Complicating the struggle that church members have with conflict is the anger that is so often present in conflict situations. Anger usually arises because people feel frustrated in meeting their objectives. Anger is a natural response to frustration. Discovering that one is angry is not necessarily a moral problem, but how one deals with that anger is definitely a moral issue. In Matt. 5:21-22 Jesus is quoted as saying: "Do not commit murder; anyone who commits murder must be brought to judgment. But what I tell you is this: Anyone who nurses anger against his brother must be brought to judgment" (NEB). St. Paul in Eph. 4:26-27 wrote: "Be angry, but do not sin; do not let the sun go down on your anger, and give no opportunity to the devil." The point of both these passages is identical. The problem is not the anger. The problem is that sinful human beings tend to reflect upon, emphasize, propagate, encourage, and nurture anger to the point where it becomes all-consuming. The anger itself, if confronted and worked through, does not necessarily lead to the wounds which uncontrolled anger can produce.

When one gets beyond the point of simply ignoring conflict, or feeling a sense of panic because a conflict has developed, and begins to recognize that conflict is not only inevitable between members of Christian congregations but also can provide the climate for thinking through an issue, then some positive developments can transpire. Members of congregations should understand that Christians can easily mix their personal goals with what they perceive to be congregational goals. Sometimes personal goals and congregational goals are mutually exclusive! In addition, there may be organizational goals or denominational goals which conflict with the institutional goals of individual members. Therefore in every congregation there are literally hundreds of individuals whose goals for the congregation are very important to them as individuals. Many church leaders are surprised when seemingly uninvolved or apathetic members of congregations attend meetings because specific congregational concerns interest them. Since even the most loosely attached members have personal goals for their congregation which they want to see it attain, they react when they see the attainment of those goals threatened. When such a reaction happens, a conflict situation has arisen.

Members may also have other personal goals which on the surface have nothing to do with their church, yet those personal goals can affect their behavior in the church. Examples of personal goals might be to be elected or appointed to a position of leadership, to persuade the congregation to buy property insurance from the company the person represents, or to serve as soloist in the choir. If the attainment of these goals is frustrated, the person may foment conflict.

Thus there are three types of goals that compete with one another within congregations. First, there are the goals that people have for themselves, and the local congregation is viewed as a means to attain these goals. The second set of goals are the personal goals that individuals have for the congregation as an organization. The third set of goals are those that are identified as those of the congregation or of the denomination.[45] Conflict develops between the members within congregations because the specifics of these goals can be contradictory and mutually exclusive of one another.[46]

Obviously the congregations which are likely to experience the least amount of conflict situations are those which are composed of members who share a high level of conformity relative to individual personal goals, personal institutional goals, and institutional goals.[47] This is one of the reasons why the homogeneous unit concept as highlighted in Church Growth literature works effectively, at least at one level. Homogeneous units usually are afflicted with less conflict than heterogeneous units. Yet it would be a complete misunderstanding to suggest that homogeneous units are not prone to any conflict. The conflicts that do arise, however, will generally not be conflicts concerning issues like race, language, or class differences.[48]

Theorists who study conflict and have developed strategies to cope with it often talk or write about the creative use of conflict.[49] This means that as a congregation gets to a point in its history where conflict arises, the congregation needs to help its members manage the conflict so that through the process of resolving it the members will: (1) experience emotional and spiritual growth, (2) discover new relationships and alternatives to solve the causes of the conflict, and (3) develop a sense of real cohesiveness and unity.

There are some principles which are very important to apply if conflict is to be managed in a creative way. Lewis suggests seven:

1. Church leaders can be useful in helping congregations manage conflict when the leaders are able to help the members of the congregation feel good about themselves as individuals and as a congregation.[50]

2. Creative conflict management depends on the ability of people to listen to what others are saying. Such listening takes seriously the need to recognize that people speak out of their own experiences. These experiences make them unique as persons.[51]

3. Conflicts are often fueled because people do not examine their own assumptions about the nature of given situations.[52] Examining assumptions is no small task. One of the reasons that assumptions are so difficult to confront is the very fact that they are assumptions. People generally assume that their assumptions are givens which do not need to be tested or examined.

4. Conflicts are aggravated because people often do not know what they wish to accomplish. Determining the objectives or goals in specified situations in congregations is an important step in resolving conflicts.[53]

5. Conflict cannot be managed effectively if it is impossible to identify the primary issue that caused the conflict. Every party in a conflict situation needs to agree on what the issue is that has created the conflict.[54] Until this step is achieved much heat but very little light will be generated.

6. Once the issue has been identified, it is time to look for the possible alternatives that are available so that all parties in the conflict can feel that their needs and concerns have been met.[55]

Authors have suggested various ways to resolve conflicts. One approach is to talk about the four c's, namely: capitulation, compromise, coexistence, and collaboration. The first three ways to resolve conflict— capitulation, compromise, and coexistence—by definition do not give the conflicting parties the feeling that their needs and concerns have been met. However, in the collaborative approach to resolving conflicts most, if not all, of the needs and concerns of the conflicting parties are addressed. Collaborative efforts at conflict resolution are initially time-consuming, but the collaborative approach saves time in the long run because people will feel that the conflict has really been resolved, and they are enabled to feel good about themselves, their fellow members, and the resolution that was developed.[56]

7. Finally, the process of managing conflicts should be adopted by the congregation for use at the required times and should not be re-created or reinvented each time a crisis develops.[57] If a particular process is identified and institutionalized at a time when conflict is not apparent, then when the process is needed later and is applied, conflicting parties are less likely to feel that the process was designed to get them to conform, but rather that the previously agreed-upon process is as objective a way to confront the conflict as subjective people are able to create.[58]

Lewis proposes that congregational conflict management should be placed into the context of liturgy. He has written:

The elements of this liturgy intentionally parallel a Christian liturgy for worship.

Thanksgiving: I am an intentional person created by God with goals and a purpose. . . .

Confession: I seek the fulfillment of my goals, even at the cost of the well-being of others and myself.

Absolution: God affirms and loves me in spite of the destructiveness of my will and actions.

Intercession: Because I experience affirmation and transformation, I am open to and care for the needs and goals of others.

Service: I will invest my creative energy in the midst of conflict to search for alternatives that lead to the fulfillment and wholeness of all persons.[59]

## Retention Through Encouragement of Volunteers

People who feel good about their involvement as volunteers in the life of the congregation are also people who drop out less frequently. As indicated in chapter one, some people who drop out of a congregation's life do so because they feel used. Seemingly the issue is not how many hours one spends in volunteer work but how one feels about the work. People who feel positive about what they have done and who receive positive feedback from others about what they have done are less likely to drop out.[60]

This observation is supported by evidence from empirical studies which suggest that on the average the members of congregations who feel they are encouraged and enabled to influence how the congregation carries on its affairs will feel more satisfaction than those who are unable to exert such influence.[61]

## Retention Through Increased Congregational Warmth

Another group of people who tend to remain active are those who work in professions or occupations which make it necessary to meet and work with strangers.[62] In a time of high mobility some people cope well with their own mobility and the mobility of others. Their personality, training, and experiences do not limit them to a relatively small circle of lifelong friends. Such people are more likely to be stayers in a congregation's life, for they are able to adjust to things, particularly the changing nature of fellow members. If indeed people who are willing to meet strangers are more likely not to drop out, their very willingness may be a real help to those who do not have the ability to meet strangers. The 1978 Gallup data indicated that unchurched people were more likely than churched people to agree with the statement that the church is "not warm or accepting of outsiders."[63]

## Retention Through Responsible Social Action

Congregations that wish to retain members and continue to grow will need to provide some means for their members to be involved in social action activities.[64] This is a complicated issue because social action programming can have positive or negative effects. Some social action programming enhances commitment, while other types of programming diminish commitment.[65] For example, the congregations highlighted in *Unique Evangelical Churches*[66] all have strong programs of social ministry. The Lutheran Church—Missouri Synod has not been noted as a denomination which is highly involved in social ministry, but Missouri Synod Lutherans do have a long-standing commitment in special education, particularly with deaf and handicapped people. More recently LCMS congregations have responded positively to sponsoring refugees from Southeast Asia, providing day care services for working parents who need loving care for their preschool children, and encouraging members to become donors of body organs by completing and carrying on their persons organ transplant donor cards. These activities have allowed Lutherans to give expression to their personal concerns about people who are less fortunate than they.

## Summary

Genuine concern for the spiritual well-being of fellow members is the primary motivation which causes congregations to take seriously the need to try to prevent their members from becoming inactive. Such concern for fellow members of the body of Christ is an outgrowth of the Gospel message. Because of God's love, which is conveyed to us in the

Gospel, we who are forgiven and beloved people of God are empowered to love all the other people whom God also loves. To reflect God's love for us by loving others is an important part of the Christian life.

At the same time God has made His body here on earth responsible for ministry in His behalf. God has given us minds to assist us in analyzing what is happening around us. Because of the insights provided to us by empirical studies conducted by social scientists, we have an increasingly accurate perception of how specific factors contribute to or detract from people's participation in the life of parishes. Many of these factors can be influenced and even controlled by the leaders and members of the local congregation. What is needed is the willingness of congregations to take decisive action in regard to these factors so that fewer people will feel nudged toward inactivity.

# Chapter 3

# Attitudes Toward Inactives

Even if congregations employ all of the strategies suggested in chapter 2 to minimize the number of their members who become dropouts, no system will assure that all members remain active. Therefore congregations also have to be prepared to minister to members who have become inactive. Preventive action is dependent upon a mind-set that values taking preventive measures. Most church leaders have the heart for preventive action, but many of these same leaders have less heart for confronting inactives.

That very same emotional response immobilizes many church leaders and sets up interpersonal dynamics which doom to failure many attempts to visit with inactive members and work through the concerns they have. This emotional response carries with it some unhelpful stereotypes about inactives—assumptions about who they are, what motivates them, how they might best be confronted, and even a priori conclusions about why visiting them is not productive. Therefore, prior to suggesting a plan or program of calling on inactives, the issue of stereotypes and assumptions must be addressed.

Gerhard Knutson, in his book *Ministry to the Inactives*, has prepared a chart that presents the stereotypes which active church members have over against the inactive and vice versa. The chart also attempts to describe how individuals from each group feel as they confront representatives from the opposite group. As one reflects upon these data it does not take an expert in human relationships to understand why there are difficulties when actives and inactives speak with one another.

| "Actives" | | LABELS, STEREOTYPES BARRIERS, MISUNDERSTANDINGS | "Inactives" | |
|---|---|---|---|---|
| How they see "Inactives" | How they feel | | How they see "Actives" | How they feel |
| dropouts | frustrated | | hypocrites | condemned |
| delinquents | fearful | | do-gooders | forgotten |
| do-nothings | anxious | | nosy | left out |
| inactive | worried | | fussy | lonely |
| lazy | hostile | | nitpickers | rejected |
| backsliders | suspicious | | bossy | abandoned |
| sinners | full of pity | | "in group" | angry |
| complainers | sympathetic | | judges | suspicious |
| excuse makers | puzzled | | high & mighty | having failed |
| | embarrassed | | meddlers | apathetic |
| | | | | no longer caring[1] |

Individuals in both groups have developed stereotypes which project on members of the opposite group a great deal of negative baggage. Words like "dropouts, delinquents, do-nothings, inactive, lazy, backsliders, sinners, complainers, excuse makers" are heavily negative, reflecting feelings of disdain, judgment, and even hostility. They are words which suggest that Law is being applied. Perhaps Law needs to be applied in specific situations, but it needs to be applied properly. Using Law to motivate people to a sanctified response is a confusion of Law and Gospel. Law can only produce rebellion, false piety, or despair.[2] It is no wonder that when Law is applied improperly, as seems so frequently to be the case, the inactives rebel.

The list of words Knutson uses to describe how the actives feel includes words which indicate that many active people do not understand the proper application of Law and Gospel. Their emotional state seems much more like the elder brother's than that of the waiting, forgiving father in Jesus' parable of the prodigal son (Luke 15:11-32). Perhaps the word "sympathetic" is the only one which conveys a relatively positive and nonjudgmental meaning.

Active people may be genuinely concerned about the spiritual welfare of the inactive people, but all too frequently the issue, from the vantage point of the inactives, is that active members want to make certain the congregation can continue to meet its financial and other commitments. From this perspective the inactives feel that they are means to an end rather than ends in themselves.

At the same time, inactives have perceptions about active members which are equally judgmental. The connotations of the words used by inactives to describe actives all have negative loadings. The attitudes behind such words effectively destroy any evaluation of the actives which would consider their behavior as being motivated by genuine concern about the spiritual well-being of the inactives.

Because of the connotations attached to the words "condemned, rejected, and having failed," which Knutson has selected to describe how inactives feel about themselves, it is apparent that the inactives have felt the judgment of both God's law and the judgmental opinions of active members. Inactives also experience other feelings which serve to diminish their personal concepts of self-worth.

It is clear from all the data presented earlier in this book that inactives cannot be stereotyped. Inactives are not a single homogeneous group, and this generalization is also true of the active members of congregations. Thus, leaders of congregations will need to expend the necessary effort to counteract the inclination of active and inactive members to stereotype themselves and one another.

Lyle Schaller has prepared 15 assumptions which he feels active members and leaders of congregations should possess when they confront inactive members. It is Schaller's contention that scapegoating, which is so common among active members, is not productive.[3] His assumptions also speak directly to the stereotyping of active and inactive members discussed above.

Schaller suggests the following 15 assumptions.

1. We assume that every person who united with this congregation did so with complete sincerity and in good faith.[4]

Donald Metz has reported that charter members and other long-term members of congregations often suspect that newer members are not as dedicated to the congregation as they were when they joined.[5] Older members recall the many hours of planning and labor that went into building the church, gathering members, and providing a firm financial base for the congregation. They think about how in the early days of the congregation they often did double or triple duty by serving on various boards or committees and how they contributed beyond their financial means. These people evaluate newer members' contributions of time, talent, and treasure to be less intense or expansive or sacrificial than their own. They can even resent that the newer members seem to take for granted the fruits of others people's labors.

This observation on the part of Metz helps to illustrate the problem. Christian people are to reflect the light that has come to them from Jesus Christ. But the issue remains, how is that light to be reflected? What are the fruits of faith to look like? Seemingly long-term members frequently conclude that the fruits of faith should exhibit themselves in actions which are supportive of the congregation as an organization. If such a conclusion is indeed the criterion by which new members are judged, it is easy to understand why new and older members talk past one another.

Schaller suggests in his first statement that each member should assume that every other member joined the congregation sincerely with the purpose of being faithful to the congregation and faithful to God.

Some congregations have tried to develop measures by which leaders can evaluate the illusive category called "faithfulness." Elizabeth O'Connor, in her book *Call to Commitment*, described the approach of The Church of the Savior, Washington, D.C., as that congregation's leaders attempted to insure the integrity of church membership by asking converts to commit themselves to study, spiritual discipline, and Christian service[6] prior to their being accepted into the membership of the congregation.

The approach of The Church of the Savior and the programs of many other parishes which are similar to that of this famous congregation located in the nation's capital seem to provide specific criteria to assist in encouraging a common understanding about what actions, behaviors, and attitudes constitute "faithfulness" on the part of members. But there are ripple effects from that very specificity. Specificity demands that more bookkeeping must be done to keep track of members' involvement. Inherent in the process may be a built-in bias emphasizing the survival goals of the congregation. At minimum, the selection of the criteria needs to be done most carefully, for the chosen criteria become determinative and not just evaluative.

   2. We assume that every person who united with this congregation and is now an inactive member has what is, from their point of view, a good reason for being inactive.[7]

Schaller's second assumption is built upon data similar to those which have been set forth earlier in this book. The assumption takes seriously the feelings and perceptions of the persons who have become inactive. The statement avoids the tendency of church leaders and active lay persons to stereotype inactive members as "delinquents, backsliders, and excuse makers." The statement recognizes that there are a variety of reasons that persons might have which nudged them to inactivity. Since the reasons are judged as "good," there is inherent in the statement an implied acceptance of the real reasons people offer for becoming inactive. Implied also seems to be willingness to confront and overcome those good reasons so that inactive members can be assisted to become active again.

3. We assume that if each inactive member has a good reason for being inactive they will continue to be inactive until after that reason has been identified and eliminated.[8]

So frequently the assumption of active persons is that the inactive person has "let down" the congregation as a whole and individual friends in particular. However, Schaller's third assumption not only reaffirms the thought that an inactive person feels he has a good reason for becoming inactive, but he also has a good reason to stay inactive until that reason is dealt with by the congregation. Thus, instead of the active members emphasizing being "let down" by the inactive member, active members need to develop the awareness that inactive members feel that the congregation has "let them down." Therefore active members are put on notice that, instead of expecting inactive people to do something, they as active members may well need to do something before the inactives can be activated.

4. We assume that for us to speculate and attempt to identify that reason will be less productive than seeking to discover that reason more directly by talking with the inactive member.[9]

Countless fruitless hours are spent by committees, boards, and church councils in discussions trying to identify the reasons why certain people do not wish to participate any longer in the total life of the parish. These discussions are fruitless simply because the people who are inactive have usually not been asked why they have become inactive. Broad generalizations like "people are more secular now," "times are not tough enough," "what we need is a good depression and people will come flocking back to church," "ours is an age of apathy," "people do not get involved in anything anymore," and "people are just too busy, they do not have their priorities straight," are heard in these discussions. As the data in chapter 1 clearly demonstrates, inactivity is usually caused by more specific problems, issues, difficulties in relationships, etc. Broad generalizations miss the mark. They do not provide helpful analysis.

Schaller's implied advice is so simple and logical that there seems to be no other alternative. Yet responses from the leadership of local parishes might well indicate that less than half the Christian congregations in the United States consciously seek out and listen to individuals who have become inactive in order to discern from them the reasons that have motivated these former members to become inactive.

5. We assume that since all our inactive members are normal human beings they will respond like other normal human beings and offer excuses rather than reasons when we first approach them. (If we accept their excuses as reasons or if we try to dismiss these excuses as unimportant, we may never discover the real reasons behind the excuses.)[10]

This assumption is built upon the findings of individuals who work with the theoretical concepts revolving around the theme of "defensive communication."

People become defensive when they perceive that they are somehow under attack. The person who is on the defensive "thinks about how he appears to others, how he may be seen more favorably, how he may win, dominate, impress, or escape punishment, and/or how he may avoid or mitigate a perceived or an anticipated attack."[11]

The defensive response of the receiver of a message can also produce defensiveness in the sender of the message. As the receiver becomes increasingly defensive "he becomes less and less able to perceive accurately the motives, the values, and the emotions of the sender."[12]

Defensive climates include situations in which the receivers feel that the senders are: (a) evaluating them, (b) attempting to control them, (c) employing a strategy involving ambiguous and multiple motivations, (d) being dishonest by acting as if they are neutral, (e) giving the impression of being superior in one or more ways over against the receivers and by (f) being certain of the "rightness" of their cause.[13]

Since they feel defensive, inactive members tend to offer excuses for being absent from the worship services and activities of the congregation. The excuses are designed to help the persons on the defensive alter how they appear to others, place themselves in a more favorable light, provide a means to escape punishment, and blunt any attack that is forthcoming from the active members who are making the visit.

However, it is possible to set a more helpful context for discussions. In this more helpful and supportive context the active members will attempt to emphasize descriptive speech rather than evaluative judgments, a problem-solving approach rather than control, spontaneity rather than manipulative strategies, empathy rather than a false neutrality, equality rather than a sense of superiority, and openness rather than certainty.[14]

Such a positive context will cause the inactive members to be less defensive and less likely to offer excuses in the first place. However, the very fact that they are being called upon as inactive members will no doubt create some defensiveness. That defensiveness will produce excuses. It is imperative that those excuses be heard and taken seriously, but the excuses must be recognized as not being the real reasons for the inactivity of the inactive members. Those real reasons will surface, if they are to be expressed at all, much later in the series of conversations.

In this context it is important to note that when the Gallup interviewers asked inactive church members what could possibly cause them to return to their churches, they most frequently responded that they would return if someone could help them confront their doubts and assist them to find faith.[15] This often-used response of Gallup's subjects suggests that when inactives are not made to feel defensive and when they are provided with settings in which they can share their vulnerabilities, they often are asking the "right questions" and seeking the "right information." When provided with such an opportunity, faithful people can share what Jesus Christ has come to mean to them. A detailed exposition of the message to be shared is found in Robert Kolb's *Theology for Evangelism*, published as part of this series of monographs.

   6. We assume that we can learn more by listening than by talking, and therefore our approach to our inactive members will be one of active listening. We can expect this to require at least several hours of active listening with each inactive member or inactive family.[16]

In another of his books, titled *Hey, That's Our Church*, Schaller explains what he means by listening. It is imperative that the callers simply listen to what members being visited have to say about their life in the congregation. Schaller suggests that the simple question which might be asked is, "How are things going with you?" He stresses that callers should not fall into the trap of interviewing the persons being called upon by asking a series of defensive questions or feeling the need to agree or disagree with the statements offered by the persons being visited.[17]

The callers merely listen carefully to all that is being said, so that the persons being visited perceive the genuine interest the callers have in them.

The concept of active listening was popularized by Thomas Gordon in his books and in the Parent Effectiveness Training workshops his organization has developed and sponsored. Theoretically, Gordon is dependent on the writings of the famous counselor Carl Rogers. Active listening implies "feeding back" to the speaker what the listener understands the speaker has said, without judgment or interpretation. The active listening process is designed to allow the speaker to say what needs to be said, and then the speaker has the opportunity to hear back from someone else what the speaker said initially. The process helps the speaker clarify thoughts and feelings, helps the listener perceive what the speaker wishes to say, and assures the speaker that the thoughts and feelings being spoken are being heard and taken seriously.

    7. We assume this listening process is more likely to require six to ten hours, rather than two or three hours, if we are serious about getting beyond the veneer of excuses and discovering the basic reasons why this member is now inactive.[18]

In this assumption Schaller is pleading that individuals who visit inactive members will: (1) listen carefully, (2) be ready to expend numerous hours on a given person or family, (3) be patient enough and listen long enough to discover what are the real reasons which have caused the members to become inactive.

Most people are well aware of behaviors which are helpful in facilitating the listening process and those which are not. National magazines as widely diversified in content and readership as *Nation's Business,*[19] *U. S. News and World Report,*[20] *Current Health,*[21] *Redbook,*[22] and *Christianity Today*[23] have included articles about listening over the past few years of publication.

Personal experiences with groups of adults and young people who have not been enrolled in high school or college courses in communications theory or who have not read articles in the popular magazines available on newsstands have demonstrated that they can develop lists of behaviors which assist or hinder the listening process. Therefore one can assume that normal adults instinctively draw conclusions about how effectively they are being heard by the people who are listening to them. One observable behavior is for listeners to give speakers the time necessary for them to communicate their messages completely. That is the reason why Schaller includes the necessity of being willing to spend the time needed to hear.

    8. We assume this process will probably require several visits, and it is unlikely to be accomplished in one or two visits. (Frequently the first visit produces a series of excuses and guilt responses by the inactive member, the second visit releases a variety of hostile comments, and not until the third or fourth visit is the caller able to hear the basic reasons why this person is now inactive.)[24]

If the assumption is correct that it will normally take six to ten hours of conversation to enable dropouts to express the real reasons why they have dropped out of parish life, it is logical to assume that it will take three or four visits at the homes of dropouts before the process can completely unfold.

Inherent in assumption number eight are a number of warnings about pitfalls that callers should try to avoid when making calls on inactive members.

The first pitfall has to do with the way callers handle the excuses the dropouts offer. That concern was presented above. The second has to do with the hostile comments that may arise on the second visit. During these visits it is important for the callers not to respond defensively. To respond defensively is to make communication more problematic and perhaps assure that the real reasons for dropping out will never surface. Third, once the real reasons for dropping out become known, those reasons have to be taken seriously and addressed adequately.

9. We assume that the longer we wait after a member has become inactive, the more difficult it will be to help that person become an active member of the congregation.[25]

In his research John Savage discovered that the dropouts represented in his sample population unconsciously gave their local congregations six- to eight-week deadlines for inquiring about their absence at church. Schaller had this information in mind when he composed this particular assumption.[26]

Leaders of large congregations with multiple staff arrangements know how easy it is for people "to slip between the cracks," and how some people can be absent for months or even years before they are discovered to be among the missing.

This assumption also helps to explain some of the hostility and hurt that bubbles out from dropouts when callers from their former congregation visit them many months after they have dropped out. The dropouts' reactions seem to imply that they are feeling something like, "Big deal, it sure took you people long enough to discover our absence and to come and inquire about us. If we are so valuable or important to the life of the congregation, why didn't you visit us much sooner?"

By implication it can be concluded that every congregation has to design some means to keep track of all its people. Whether the approach selected is the "rite of friendship ritual,"[27] attendance cards, shepherding arrangements, cluster groups, a buddy system, or some other approach is immaterial. What is important is that the system selected be both efficient and effective.

10. We assume that few, if any, of the existing classes, circles, organizations, and face-to-face groups in this congregation are

completely effective in caring for the members of that class or group, in listening and responding constructively to their hurts, anxieties, and concerns, or in being sensitive to the needs of persons not in that class or group. Therefore we need a backup system to reach and minister to the people who are not cared for by the face-to-face groups, or we will always be faced with the problem of inactive members.[28]

Findings of studies are available which suggest that dropouts often cite frustrations in relationships and interpersonal conflicts as major reasons why they have dropped out of parish life. Although individuals rarely list presently satisfying relationships or hoped-for relationships as reasons for joining congregations, broken or frustrated relationships are often identified as creating problems which cause them to leave a congregation. The "Church Growth" literature is filled with admonitions that congregations take seriously the importance of small groups to better meet the spiritual and emotional needs of members. Schaller has also emphasized the importance of face-to-face groups in congregations.[29] Such face-to-face groups are particularly important in highly mobile, nonethnic congregations located in urban areas.

Schaller's assumption quoted above implies how important small sharing groups are in the life of the church. But what is more, Schaller concludes that no matter how many or how effective the groups in a congregation are, there will be individuals who will find that their needs are not met by the groups that exist. Therefore every congregation needs to have some congregational group that has as its objective the meeting of unmet needs in a systematic, programmed manner. Schaller judges that congregations without such backup plans will produce a continuing list of dropouts.

11. We assume that the person who has become inactive often has greater difficulty in coping with feelings of helplessness, hopelessness, anger, hostility, anxiety, or neglect than do the more active members of the congregation. Therefore it is of critical importance that (a) the inactive member be called on before these feelings have become deeply ingrained and (b) that the caller have the personality and skills which will *not* further intensify and enhance these feelings of inadequacy and guilt but will rather help the inactive member overcome these feelings.[30]

Schaller's eleventh assumption is based on the conclusions that John Savage has drawn from his research using subjects from Methodist congregations. The research model that Savage designed was suggested by findings from other studies which had addressed issues such as anxiety, anger, helplessness, hopelessness, apathy, and boredom.[31] Savage discovered that when the anxiety-anger level of his subjects had become too intense they began to manifest behavior such as not attending worship services, absenting themselves from committee meetings at church, and ceasing to include religious language in their conversations.[32]

Such behavior signals that these people are potential dropouts. Given the nature and intensity of these people's feelings, it is imperative that each congregation have within it both an informal structure which manifests itself in members genuinely caring about one another as they minister to one another's spiritual, emotional, and physical needs and a formal structure to make certain that no individual member's needs are left unmet or ignored.

Active members who make calls on potential dropouts must recognize how deeply troubled and frustrated the potential dropouts really are. The callers need to possess the skills of helping the persons who are dropping out confront the various negative feelings they possess.

12. We assume that the vast majority of inactive members send a signal to the church when they experience an anxiety-producing conflict or sense of helplessness. If this signal is ignored, the member may enter into a period of inactivity to further test "whether anyone really cares about me." After the end of this test or probationary period that person becomes an increasingly rigid, inactive member. Therefore it is very important that (a) every congregation have some system for identifying the early signals sent to the church by the potentially inactive member and (b) a system for quickly responding to these signals, such as a cadre of trained callers who regularly make listening calls.[33]

As noted earlier, Savage found that the potential dropouts gave their fellow members six to eight weeks to notice that they were moving out of the mainstream of congregational life. If the dropouts were not confronted by clergy, leaders, or active members of their congregation, they began to find other activities to fill the void left in their individual lives.[34] This waiting period allows the people to take stock of the grief they feel in parting from the fellowship and provides a means to determine if anyone is concerned enough about them to visit them.[35] Ultimately the people who internalize their problems are described by Savage as bored dropouts while those who blame others for their difficulties are described as apathetic dropouts.[36]

The six to eight weeks that individuals give their congregation to notice their inactivity is judged to be adequate by those becoming inactive but is a frighteningly brief period for those who provide leadership in a congregation. Mobility of members, sheer numbers of people in some congregations, resistance on the part of members to "taking weekly attendance at worship services," and other factors make it difficult to identify the persons who are dropping out within the relatively short time span of six to eight weeks.

As suggested earlier, it is obvious that congregations must have some accurate yet generally acceptable means to monitor the church attendance of all their members and to gauge the involvement of members in their auxiliary organizations. Diminishing involvement in worship and in attendance at the meetings of congregational committees and organizations are early signals that persons are potential dropouts.

But such information is worthless if it is only gathered; the congregation must act on it. One way to make use of the data is to have groups of trained callers who specialize in following up on the potential dropouts to hear them out and deal with their feelings in constructive ways so that they will want to return to active life in the congregation.

13. We assume that the spiritual needs of some members change as the years go by. Therefore some of our longtime members who may appear to have become inactive or who are shopping for a new church home should be identified not as bored or apathetic or hostile or disinterested but rather as potential graduates from our congregation. These are the persons who have benefited from everything our congregation has been able to offer them, and as graduates are seeking a postgraduate level of challenge in terms of their own personal religious experience and discipline. If our church cannot or does not offer this, they will look elsewhere. . . . A constructive response is for the congregation to be prepared to offer a new and varied assortment of events and experiences for the personal and spiritual growth of the members.[37]

This assumption is based on the results of a study done by John F. Biersdorf. The individuals from whom Biersdorf obtained information represented a selected group of Roman Catholic, Protestant, and Jewish congregations. Biersdorf used a variety of instruments to gather data for analysis. He found that the people in his sample had a much higher average score on a Biblical knowledge test than the average score produced by a national sample. In commenting on all these test results Biersdorf wrote of the people in his sample population:

. . .they seem to be more like graduates of the traditional religious groups. They have learned and practiced the faith, and in many cases they have found their way to positions of leadership and have given long service. If these people now struggle to find new symbols to express their faith, or experiment with novel communities that do not fit into established institutions, it may be because traditional communities have failed. It may be because they did too good a job.[38]

The concept which undergirds this assumption is hard for many members and leaders of congregations to accept. For many the suggestion that some members have experienced so much spiritual growth that they have graduated from their congregation implies that the original congregation is too limited. This implication is perceived to be a negative evaluation of the congregation. Pastors of such congregations may have struggled to provide experiences to facilitate such spiritual growth on the part of some members. Just about the time these pastors expect these members to have become significant assets in their ministries, these carefully cultivated individuals demonstrate their coming of age spiritually by moving on. Pastors experience feelings of rejection, frustration, negative evaluation, and a whole host of other emotions. Such pastors often express these feelings in unhelpful ways when they confront the graduates from their congregations.

The very word "graduate" is meant to imply a neutral meaning. People graduate from elementary school, high school, college, and master's and doctoral programs. In such settings graduation is looked upon as a sign of achievement. Generally teachers do not begrudge the fact that students graduate. However, most pastors and congregational leaders are not as likely to perceive graduation of members in the same neutral sense.

There are at least two possible responses to the reality of graduation. Schaller suggests that congregations faced with graduate dropouts might want to expand their programs so that they might continue to provide a setting in which members may do "postgraduate work." This option might provide a real morale booster to other dedicated lay persons in those congregations and could provide exciting challenges to the professional leadership.

A second alternative for congregations is to continue to do "business as usual," recognizing that specific congregations cannot be all things to all people. Such an approach would take seriously the nature of the initial nurturing role such congregations play in the lives of people, but that limitations are realities, and therefore congregations should rejoice over the fact that they have produced graduates who have been enabled to grow to the point of moving on to a more enriched spiritual environment.

14. We assume that in establishing meaningful communication with inactive members we are faced with two challenges. One is to

63

listen (see item 6 above). The second is to be aware of the assumptions we bring to the conversation with the inactive member and to recognize which of our assumptions may be counterproductive.[39]

The issue of listening has been addressed above. To listen effectively is difficult, yet the skill must be developed. But perhaps even more difficult is to be able to be aware of the feelings that active and inactive members have over against one another. These feelings were discussed at some length earlier in this chapter.

15. Finally, we assume that while we do not have direct control over all the many factors that may cause a member to be inactive, we do have complete and direct control over the assumptions on which we build our response to the inactive member as well as over what we do or do not do that causes members to become inactive.[40]

Chapter 1 clearly demonstrated that many factors can contribute to producing inactivity. Some of those factors—like mixed marriages, the movement of company executives every few years, changes in racial and ethnic compositions of neighborhoods, displacements of populations through urban renewal and the building of expressways, to name a few examples—are items about which local congregations have little or no control. However, as congregations address these and many other factors promoting inactivity, congregations have complete control over the assumptions they use to develop their responses to inactive members as well as to address those specifics in the congregation's life that cause people to become inactive.

Therefore, rather than lamenting and wringing their collective hands over those variables they cannot control, congregations need to take charge and identify and address directly those things over which they do exercise control.

Even though the primary reason for being interested in activating the inactives is theological, it needs to be pointed out that empirical evidence suggests that a significant number of inactive people wish to have their spiritual needs addressed by the Gospel.

Based on the data generated by the 1978 Gallup study, numbers of authors have suggested that among the many dropouts there is a rather large group of individuals who seem to be open to church membership but who have not been attracted to conservative Protestant churches. The dropouts who are potential prospects for reactivation are cosmopolitan-modernist people who could be attracted to congregations whose theological perspectives are capable of helping them relate the Christian faith to the lives they lead and the roles they play in the line-staff relationships of corporations and the give and take of public service. They probably will not respond to a theological perspective which is limited to addressing what is happening to them in their private and family experiences.[41] Some mainline denominations and local congregations need to identify these would-be seekers and design strategies to address their spiritual needs.

Once congregations have helped pastors and lay callers and leaders to eliminate from their thoughts and vocabulary concepts and words which stereotype individuals and which are based upon faulty assumptions about who inactives are and how they should be ministered to, it is imperative that all members be helped to respond helpfully to the inactives when they return.

It is important to note that many former dropouts express the feeling that, upon returning, they are not accepted by their fellow church members.[42] These feelings reported by former inactive members may be based on some highly subjective data, yet it would be a mistake to ignore them. People act on the basis of their perceptions, whether their feelings are based on "objective" or "subjective" data.

Since it has been demonstrated that 46 percent of all Americans drop out of congregational life for at least two years of their lifetime, the issue of how active members respond to the return of the inactives will make a significant impact on whether the inactives will return to the congregation from which they have withdrawn. Since it has also been demonstrated that 80 percent of these dropouts eventually do return to active church life, the importance of the response of the actives to the return of the inactives is clearly evident.[43]

Because formerly inactive members, who have returned to active participation in the congregation, have gone through experiences similar to those being faced by the recent returnees, some congregations have encouraged such returnees to be very active in ministry to inactives and recent returnees. Such members generally possess a sensitivity which exceeds that of the members who have always been active.[44]

The primary message of this chapter can best be summarized with the word "attitude." The attitude church members have about the inactive members of the congregation will influence how they view, approach, listen to, respond to, and encourage their former fellow church members who are coming back to involvement and activity. Any organized programs designed to address the needs and concerns of inactive members will probably be ineffective if the programs do not seriously consider and strive to adjust the attitudes of the active members who serve as visitors and the attitudes of the rank and file members of the congregation, who will need to be prepared to welcome the returning members with open arms.

# Chapter 4

# Church Discipline

The previous chapter emphasized the importance of positive congregational attitudes when ministering to people who are becoming inactive. But this should not be perceived as implying that there is no role for church discipline in working with inactive people. Responsible application of church discipline has an important role to play in the caring ministry that should be applied to inactive members. Characteristics and qualities of such responsible church discipline are the major components of this chapter.

Any attempt to talk about church discipline in the modern context is fraught with the difficulties that are always present when a complex issue is being explored. Those difficulties are increased because most pastors, church leaders, and laity already have strong feelings about the subject of church discipline. Church discipline is a controversial theological issue, and any discussion of church discipline quickly demonstrates that there are many opinions concerning what constitutes a Biblical understanding of it.

The polarity which exists within the modern church on the subject of church discipline is represented by one view which holds that loving concern for fellow Christians necessitates that no discipline at all is to be exercised in the church. The purveyors of this view posit that the church ought to be such a loving environment that there is no place for law. The only legitimate proclamation is the proclamation of Gospel.

The proponents of the position which occupies the opposite pole on the spectrum suggest that discipline is a mandatory activity of the church. But because some proponents of this view have at times included items like long hair worn by men, dancing, recreational playing of cards, use of musical instruments, and a whole host of other behaviors among the items that demand disciplinary action, some people have come to view church discipline as being generally legalistic and/or moralistic.

The Biblical position on church discipline does not drift to either side of this spectrum. The Biblical view of church discipline takes seriously both Law and Gospel and the proper distinction between Law and Gospel. This chapter will attempt to present a Biblical understanding of church discipline.

Most observers of life in congregations across the United States suggest that the practice of church discipline has fallen into disuse and has a negative reputation. The assertion has been made that there has been a significant decline in the number of discipline actions in local congregations.[1] Although it is difficult to prove conclusively that there are less discipline cases today than there were at some time in the past, there do seem to be some factors present in the lives of modern congregations which may cause discipline to be valued less.

These factors include a variety of concerns, assumptions, and judgments.

1. A more limited definition has developed over what types of actions or attitudes merit attention as discipline cases.

2. Pastors are often worn down over the years as they confront the realities of trying to apply the Biblical directives and concepts to a wide variety of specific cases.

3. There seems to be a diminished acceptance of the reality of eternal damnation. If one does not believe in eternal damnation, then there is no need to bother with discipline matters.

4. Some theologians have emphasized a definition of sin which describes sin as a condition, first and foremost. This makes it more difficult to single out specific sins which merit formal discipline proceedings.

5. Some psychologists have weakened the definition of the word "sin" by defining behavioral problems of people as emotional pathology rather than as sin.

6. Many church leaders have concluded that discipline does not work. Discipline does not change people as some other people hope it might.[2]

7. The emphasis in recent literature concerning congregations as organizations has produced a mind-set among Christians which has contributed to the demise of mutual concern and care among fellow members of congregations.

8. Many church people have few models of positive discipline to

serve as guides. As a result, such church people do not know how to "speak the truth in love" or "admonish the unruly" or "restore those caught in a fault."[3]

9. In some people's minds church discipline is linked to excommunicating church courts and intolerance. Some people reject church discipline because they believe it to be "legalism, preoccupation with externals, concern for the letter rather than the spirit of Biblical commands, authoritarian disregard for individual freedom."[4]

10. Among some people there is a feeling that application of church discipline is counterproductive.

11. Many congregations are organized around the assumption that discipline should be initiated from the "top" and be applied downward. For some the "top" may be viewed as the pastor of a congregation. For others the "top" may be a board of elders or a board of deacons. As congregations grow larger, trying to employ a practice in keeping with this assumption becomes increasingly difficult.

12. Church discipline is frustrated by the concept which one writer has called the "ecclesiological scandal."[5] This scandal has also contributed to the reluctance church people have for exercising church discipline. Just as the religious leaders of Jesus' time were scandalized by the Incarnation, which asserted that God could forgive the sins of human beings through the Man from Nazareth, so some people are scandalized when the Biblical truth is posited that Jesus has granted power to forgive and retain sins to the human beings who are the church here on earth.

13. Some see a cause in the lack of emphasis on sanctification in the preaching and teaching of many congregations. Heideman has offered the historical judgment that in recent years theologians have emphasized the "proclamation of the Gospel and the exercise of righteousness."[6] He concludes that the emphasis on proclamation and exercise of righteousness has been done at the expense of an emphasis on the sanctifying power of the Gospel. This lack of emphasis on sanctification has produced a distorted view of Christianity. This distorted view produces the paradoxical condition that people who do not understand sanctification and discipline are unable to appropriate a message of forgiveness of sins.[7]

14. Individualism within modern society tends to negate meaningful interpersonal relationships. This drive for individualism also affects people in the church. American people avoid committed relationships with other people even though they work, play, serve, and worship with those people. This kind of "wisdom of the world" is at odds with the Biblical concept of community. Community in the Biblical sense assumes

a willingness to care for the well-being of fellow believers.

Within the church there are signs that people in need of spiritual counsel and care are neglected. Many congregations provide minimal instruction for prospective members and then fail to shepherd them when they join. One distraught author has written: "There is growing evidence in the church that after a period of mutual irresponsibility and neglect, impersonally automatic procedures are concocted by which the 'dead wood members' are chopped off the membership rolls."[8]

15. Confusion exists in many congregations concerning what is the primary purpose for exercising church discipline.

Some authors reject the view that the primary purpose for church discipline is the restoration of the erring Christian brother or sister. One person has written: "We must keep in mind that the purpose of Church discipline is:

"1. To maintain the authority of Christ.
"2. To keep the purity of the Church.
"3. To save the sinful brother."[9]

Dean Kelley hypothesizes that conservative churches have grown in recent decades because they have exercised church discipline. Kelley argues that how strong an organization is depends on how membership is defined by the organization. If those membership requirements are such that they distinguish members from nonmembers and if such membership requirements are enforced by the organization, Kelley contends, such an organization will grow.

Kelley offers his observation as a sociologist of religion. It may or may not be accurate. However, when Christian writers cite Kelley's conclusion as a kind of prooftext to exhort congregational leaders to exercise church discipline, they are guilty of a major confusion of Law and Gospel. Church discipline is exercised not to make churches grow but to be careful stewards of God's people. The emphasis of Jesus is on the spiritual well-being of the individual before God.

16. The negative connotations which unfortunately have been attached to the concept of discipline have caused many, if not most, congregations to avoid situations that call for discipline. When discipline is finally used, in many congregations it is only in the most dire cases. As a result of such faulty practice the concept of "church discipline" is loaded with even more negative connotations for many people. It would be much more helpful if all the nuances of the Biblical concept of discipline could be employed regularly and consistently in the lives of all Christian congregations.[10]

Individual situations may be influenced by other considerations, but the factors listed above seem to be the most important reasons why congregations apply responsible church discipline to erring members less consistently and frequently than they should.

Perhaps the most important section of Scripture providing insight into the nature of church discipline is Matthew 18. In order to use the specific content of Matt. 18:15-18 in a responsible manner, one must study the context of these verses.

Chapter 18 begins with the disciples' question to Jesus, "Who is the greatest in the kingdom of heaven?" (18:1). Jesus responds by using a child as an illustration. ". . . unless you turn and become like children, you will never enter the kingdom of heaven" (18:3). The major point of these words is clearly that the motivation of pride which caused the disciples to ask their question is not acceptable to God. It is humility, recognizing oneself as a sinful being who is totally dependent on God's grace and forgiveness in Jesus Christ, that is a sign of greatness.

Jesus then explains that when someone receives a child, that person is actually receiving Christ Himself. On the other hand, if someone causes a child to be led astray, that person is guilty of a dreadful sin (18:5-6).

Jesus further asserts that it is of grave concern on the part of God that people not tempt others to sin or allow themselves to be tempted to sin against God; for this, unless forgiven, will lead to eternal damnation (18:7-9).

God's concern for the "little ones" is likened to the concern of a shepherd who goes to find the one sheep which has gone astray. When the shepherd finds the lost sheep, he rejoices. Jesus says that the Father is concerned, just as the shepherd was concerned, that none of his children perish spiritually (18:10-13).

Immediately after this strong word of Jesus, "So it is not the will of My Father who is in heaven that one of these little ones should perish"(18:14), we find the words of verses 15-20. This contextual setting clearly places the burden on keeping those who are "little ones" in the faith from perishing eternally. And this thrust is undergirded by the words: "If your brother listens to you, you have gained your brother" (18:15). The key word is "gained." The initial purpose of visiting with the brother is that he be gained. The purpose is not that the brother be punished or rejected.

Immediately following these crucial verses Peter is quoted as saying, "Lord, how often should my brother sin against me, and I forgive him? As many as seven times?" (18:21). The response of Jesus is once again very instructive: "I do not say to you seven times, but seventy times seven" (18:22).

71

The chapter concludes with the parable of the servant who persuades the king to forgive him his debt of ten thousand talents but who is unwilling to forgive his fellow servant his debt of a hundred denarii. The punishment of the unforgiving servant is likened to the punishment of people who do not forgive their brothers from the heart (18:23-35).

The verses following the key verses clearly highlight the need for Christian people to forgive those who have sinned and have acknowledged their need for forgiveness. To withhold forgiveness in such situations is to displease God.

Matt. 18:15 reads: "If your brother sins against you, go and tell him his fault, between you and him alone. If he listens to you, you have gained your brother." These words of Jesus have some very significant theological and practical ramifications. Church discipline needs to be personal and done in a spirit of humility (Gal. 6:1-2). It is very important to note that in Jesus' directive in Matt. 18:15-17 the first step is *personal*. Jesus uses the words "between you and him alone."

Jesus indicates that the offended person is to approach his "brother." This word choice suggests a real sense of caring and close relationship with the erring person. Because of this word choice one author has written: "This brotherly relationship begets an unselfish interest in the offender; it presupposes common ground between the one and the other; it assumes a spirit of meekness, humility, and patience; it avoids every resemblance of pride and superioity; it reveals a generous desire on the part of the one to be of help and service to the other."[11]

Jesus' directive that the person wronged should go to speak with the brother who did the wrong is helpful at a number of levels.

*First*, the brother who did the wrong has been affected by sin and is thus less likely to initiate any effort at reconciliation. Human pride and the guilt/hostility reaction make it difficult for such a person to admit his error. Because of the importance of confronting sinners with their guilt so that they might repent of what they have done, it is imperative to note that this passage is also calling all Christians who are aware of evil to confront the evildoer in their midst.

Some writers have highlighted the fact that the words "against you" in Matt. 18:15 are not found in some of the better Greek manuscripts of the New Testament.[12]

The words "against you" are also not found in Luke 17:3, Gal. 6:1-2, or James 5:19-20. The omission of the words "against you" suggests that it behooves any Christian person to approach a Christian brother or sister who has fallen into sin. A Christian does not need to wait until he/she has been offended or sit on the sidelines expecting the pastor and elders to do the confronting. It is also interesting to notice that in Matt. 5:23-26 Jesus says that the person who *committed* the offense should initiate the process of reconciliation.

Therefore the New Testament material suggests that the offender, the offended, or anyone else can start the process of church discipline! Thus the New Testament's mandate is that all of God's people are responsible for church discipline.[13]

*Second*, the person wronged is directed to go to the brother *alone*. The purpose is to avoid subjecting the brother to public ridicule or causing him to become more defensive than is absolutely necessary.

When one takes literally the directive to approach the brother individually and quietly, the possibility of gossip and character assassination will not arise. Also, this approach will assist in developing direct relationships and confidence between the parties who are talking with one another.[14]

*Third*, since the goal is to gain the brother, the context should be in keeping with that goal. The directives of Jesus keep this goal uppermost in mind. Jesus provides the constructive context of a one-to-one conversation. When such a one-to-one discussion happens in the presence of the Holy Spirit, the Lord's will becomes more sharply focused. Misunderstandings, pride, difficulties will be more easily corrected. The uniqueness of each situation can be taken into consideration in one-to-one discussions, yet the person who is struggling morally will not have to be totally dependent upon self to work through difficulties.[15]

Such a one-to-one conversation will likely be counterproductive if the offended party does not take the necessary time and expend the necessary effort in confronting the fallen brother. One of the assumptions of Lyle Schaller, which was reproduced in chapter 3, suggests that many admonition processes will take 10 to 12 hours to accomplish successfully. If the Christian who is serving as God's spokesperson in a situation is not willing to follow through on such conversations, that spokesperson might well be guilty of employing Matthew 18 mechanically—and in a spirit foreign to the will of God.

If the thought of expending 12 hours in this activity seems excessive, it is helpful to remember why Christian people serve God by confronting the erring brother. The goal is to save him from eternal damnation. Twelve hours of time given by a fellow Christian may make the difference for him for all eternity.

The hoped-for restoration of the brother assumes that the repentant brother will be forgiven. Entering into a conversation with a brother assuming he will be unrepentant or being unwilling to say words of absolution to the repentant brother is to perpetrate a great wrong. Martin Franzmann has written:

> "Forgiveness is the ground which the disciple walks on, and the air he breathes; he exists only in terms of forgiveness. . . . The disciple who will not live toward his fellow disciple by the forgiving word which he has heard from his God has forfeited the forgiving Word of God. If he violates the fellowship with the brother whom God has placed beside him, he forfeits his fellowship with God."[16]

*Fourth*, it is only after the brother has refused to repent that he is classified as no longer being a brother. Up until that point he must be respected and dealt with as a brother. The church wishes that the unrepentant person would repent and remain a brother. But since there is an unwillingness on the part of the erring brother to repent, the situation is that, "It is not that the church 'withdraws fellowship' but that it learns sadly that there is no fellowship there."[17]

But even when Jesus said that the unrepentant person was to be viewed "as a Gentile and a tax collector"(Matt. 18:17), Jesus was not saying that the person is to be ostracized. During His ministry Jesus showed special concern for the Gentiles and the tax collectors (Matt. 9:10-13; 10:3; 11:19), even though these were the groups within Jewish society who were considered to be the archtypes of evil (Matt. 5:46-47; 6:7). Yet when these people responded to Jesus' call to repentance and to His offer of grace, Jesus praised them (Matt. 21:31-32).

Therefore when Jesus asks the church to consider the unrepentant former brother a "Gentile and tax collector" He is directing the members of His body here on earth to view the lapsed brother as a mission prospect. Lapsed brothers are not to be ignored, shunned, or forgotten. They are to be evangelized.

A number of additional aspects of the Matt. 18:15-17 material need to be discussed at this point. In the first place, it is important to note that in Matt. 18:17 the word "church" does not mean individuals who are among the hierarchy. Rather the church is made up of all those people who acknowledge Jesus Christ as their Lord and Savior, and is represented by the local congregation.

Second, these passages clearly teach that when the church applies discipline it is co-judging with God. When people cite Matt. 7:1 ("Judge not, that you be not judged") as evidence that Christian people are not to be involved in Christian discipline, they are ignoring the message of Matt. 18:15-18 and also misinterpreting Matt. 7:1-5, which refers to improper, pharasaical judgments that reflect a judgmental life-style and attitude.

Third, all members of the church need to take seriously their responsibilities toward any brother or sister who has fallen into error. Perhaps that responsibility would be taken more seriously if Christian people were instructed more carefully and if they were regularly reminded of it.

For example, for 150 or so years prior to 1960 the Brethren in Christ denomination included a reference to Matt. 18:15-16 in the membership vow people took when joining a church in that denomination. New members were asked: "Do you promise that if any of your brethren or sisters should trespass against you, you will go and tell them their faults between them and you alone as taught in Matthew 18:15-16?"[18] Another question asked during the membership ceremony was: "Inasmuch as we are all fallible, if you should trespass against any of your brethren or sisters and they would come and tell you of your fault (according to Matthew 18) are you willing to receive it?"[19] Sider indicates that these references to Matthew 18 have been deleted from the membership vow used in the denomination since 1960.[20]

Fourth, inactivity on the part of brothers and sisters in Christ has to be confronted by fellow Christians. Inactivity, namely the forsaking of the means of grace, is a significant issue. Without the means of grace the Holy Spirit has no wherewithal to continue to maintain the faith of those who are absenting themselves from spiritual food.

Inactivity can be just as destructive of the Christian life as any deliberate public sin of the flesh. Therefore fellow members abdicate their responsibility to love their brothers and sisters when they are unwilling to confront the brothers and sisters who are forsaking the means of grace.

In summary it can be said that the content of Matt. 18:15-20 demands the following attitudes on the part of Christian people.

1. It is not proper for Christian people to ignore evil in the church. When evil is identified, it must be removed from the church. One way to remove the evil is to help the person who is precipitating the evil to repent and turn from the sinful activity. If that call to repentance is rejected, then the manifest sinner must be removed from the congregation.[21]

2. Christian discipline, as outlined in Matt. 18:15-18 and clarified by the surrounding verses, is not designed to simply punish or to get rid of the bad apple before it spoils all the apples in the basket.[22]

3. Christian discipline, as outlined in Matt. 18:15-18 and clarified by the surrounding verses, is designed to restore the brother to the fold. According to Jesus' parable of the lost sheep, the purpose of church

discipline is to cause the brother to be found, as the lost sheep was found, and restored to the fold.[23]

4. The motivation for Christian discipline is Christian love. Christian love is concerned about the eternal spiritual well-being of brothers and sisters in Christ. In such love there is no place for a wishy-washy approach to the reality of sin in the lives of people. When sinfulness is tolerated or excused, the law of God has been relegated to the sidelines and the Gospel message has been made useless.[24]

5. The goal of confronting the sinner is not to prove that the person who is doing the confronting is right, but to affirm that God is right. God's Word is a word of Law and of Gospel. God judges and condemns evil in His law, yet He also redeems and saves people through the Gospel. God calls upon the person who is doing the work of admonition to rightly apply that word of Law or that word of Gospel. There is no place for self-serving defensiveness on the part of God's spokesperson, or for other behaviors which confuse God's message over against sinners.[25]

6. Forsaking the means of grace that convey the power of the Gospel of Jesus Christ to Christian people is as destructive to the Christian life as any deliberate, public sin. There is no justifiable reason for ignoring the brothers and sisters who forsake the Gospel message.

A second important circumstance that must be considered in order to determine a Biblical perspective on church discipline is the situation which transpired in Corinth. A man in the congregation in Corinth was living with his stepmother as if they were husband and wife. St. Paul identifies this activity as terrible sexual immorality. The congregation in Corinth had not offered words of discipline and admonition to this couple. It is the unwillingness of the congregation to confront this problem in their midst that causes St. Paul to speak so strongly. Therefore Paul gives the following directives to the congregation in Corinth:

> I wrote to you in my letter not to associate with immoral men; not at all meaning the immoral of this world, or the greedy and robbers, or idolaters, since then you would need to go out of the world. But rather I wrote to you not to associate with anyone who bears the name of brother if he is guilty of immorality or greed, or is an idolater, reviler, drunkard, or robber—not even to eat with such a one. For what have I to do with judging outsiders? Is it not those inside the church whom you are to judge? God judges those outside. "Drive out the wicked person from among you" (1 Cor. 5:9-13).

St. Paul's argumentation in the fifth chapter of First Corinthians includes a number of emphases. St. Paul was obviously concerned about what would happen to the remainder of the members of the Corinthian congregation if the individuals were not confronted with their sinfulness. St. Paul implies that employing church discipline helps to strengthen a congregation. St. Paul was most concerned when the people of the church in Corinth did not discipline the man who was guilty of incest. St. Paul reasoned that this man's behavior was a negative influence on all the members of the church. He wrote: "Do you not know that a little leaven leavens the whole lump? Cleanse out the old leaven that you may be a new lump" (1 Cor. 5:6-7). Just as a bit of yeast affects the whole mass of dough, so the sin of the incestuous man was capable of affecting the entire congregation at Corinth. Open sin cannot be tolerated in the life of the church because of the damage it causes there. St. Paul is left with the only conclusion to the situation. He wrote: "Drive out the wicked person from among you" (1 Cor. 5:13). Thus the Biblical principle is clear that mutual care, discipline, and admonition, or the lack of these things, will affect the life of a congregation positively or negatively.[26]

But in another sense the problem facing the members of the Corinthian congregation goes beyond the concern for strengthening the congregation. St. Paul is also asserting that a public sin which is not judged or which is not confronted in the church becomes a sin of the church. When public sin is tolerated in the life of the church, that toleration involves the church in evil.[27] (See also the sin of Achan in Joshua 7:12-13.)

Paul's argumentation includes the assertion that the "old leaven," namely this sinful incest, has to be purged, and if the congregation refuses (by not exercising discipline against this pair) to purge the sin, then the sacrifice of Christ as the Passover Lamb is also impugned.

It is also clear that the message of 1 Cor. 5:11 must be interpreted to mean that the disciplining function has to be carried out by the entire congregation. This responsibility to discipline is not just the duty of church leaders.[28]

St. Paul also emphasizes, in 1 Cor. 5:12-13, that discipline must be applied to those inside the church and not against those outside the church. Even though the church can speak prophetically to every person, the jurisdiction of church discipline is limited to fellow believers only.

Even though St. Paul wanted the wicked person driven out of the congregation (1 Cor. 5:13), he also wanted the person to be brought back into the body of Christ. The purpose of driving him out was to make it possible "that his spirit may be saved in the day of the Lord Jesus" (1 Cor. 5:5). This concern on the part of St. Paul underlines the fact that there is only one primary purpose for carrying out "church discipline." That primary purpose is to bring the erring person back into the fold of God's people. When words and actions are consistent with accomplishing this primary purpose, the individual being disciplined can discern that he is the "end" in the process, not a "means" to an end.

Although the First Corinthians material also suggests that "concern for church purity, desire to protect the reputation of the church before the world, wish to bear witness to the high standards of God's righteousness through the vindication of his justice, attempt to safeguard the church against the danger of relativizing or losing its high standards,"[29] are valid concerns, these concerns are always secondary to the concern that the erring person be restored to the fellowship.

When this primary purpose is not acknowledged and when church members are not willing to accept into the fellowship of the congregation the person who is repentant, it is obvious that such Christian people misunderstand the nature and purpose of church discipline.

One illustration of this misunderstanding is evident as commentators try to decide on the identity of the offender whom Paul instructs the Corinthians to forgive in 2 Cor. 2:5-11. The church father Tertullian, early in the third century, argued that the offender was not the man who had been condemned in 1 Cor. 5:5 for his incestuous relationship. Tertullian reasoned that temporary expulsion from the Corinthian congregation, even if followed by repentance, should not be culminated by restoration of that individual to church fellowship. F. F. Bruce, a modern exegete, has written concerning the person's identity in 2 Cor. 2:5-11: "It is better to regard the offender here as someone who had been foremost in the opposition to Paul."[30]

Just who the offender in 2 Cor. 2 is may be of scholarly interest, but pinpointing his identity is probably not important. What is important to consider is the assumption of Bruce and other writers [31] who conclude, or at least seem to infer, that the offender of 2 Cor. 2 cannot be the incestuous man of 1 Cor. 5 because a sin like incest is so terrible that, even if he genuinely repented, he should not be returned to full status in the followship of the church. Therefore, based on their assumption, they make the logical deduction that St. Paul cannot be writing about the same man in 1 Cor. 5 and 2 Cor. 2. From a Lutheran vantage point such an assumption and conclusion would indicate a failure to accept or to apply the Gospel.

If indeed the man whom St. Paul urges the Corinthians to forgive in 2 Cor. 2 is the same man who was condemned for his incest in 1 Cor. 5, we can properly conclude that the preachment of Law, expressed in the judgment that as an unrepentant sinner he was to be delivered "to Satan for the destruction of the flesh" (1 Cor. 5:5), helped produce the hoped-for results. He recognized his sin. He perceived that a nonrepentant attitude on his part meant his eternal damnation. Therefore he repented. He confessed his sin. As a result of his penitence St. Paul could request that the Corinthians reaffirm their love for the individual and forgive him (2 Cor. 2:8, 10).

The directive to reaffirm their love for the repentant individual is fully in keeping with the discipline process. The motivation for executing discipline is the love that Christians have for one another. That love recognizes the need for discipline, and it recognizes the need to forgive when the disciplined sinner repents. There is no sin which cannot be forgiven except the sin of continually rejecting the forgiveness and love God makes available in Jesus Christ.

An interesting sidelight on this matter is the fact that in handling the situation in Corinth (in 2 Cor. 2:3-4, 9; 7:8, 12) Paul did not bring his apostolic clout to bear. He did not discipline or forgive the individual. Paul relied on the *congregation* to take the necessary steps! After the person was thrown out of the congregation (2 Cor. 2:6) he repented and Paul counsels the congregation to offer the repentant individual absolution (2 Cor. 2:7-10).[32]

By way of summary, the situation in Corinth caused St. Paul concern because the congregation initially abdicated its responsibility to confront the sinful individuals. This abdication meant that the congregation was being infested by sin, giving a negative witness to the world, tolerating evil, and therefore as a body was guilty of sinning, impugning the sacrifice of Jesus. The congregation also needed to be admonished because they were guilty of being unforgiving when the person ultimately repented. These same two reproaches can be laid at the doorstep of many congregations today.

In Galatians chapter 6 St. Paul teaches the importance of the restoration of fallen Christians. The efforts of Christian people to serve in a corrective manner must be carried out in gentleness and friendliness. True discipline is compassionate toward the fellow Christian who has erred. Because gentleness and friendliness must be the mind-set of the persons offering admonition, Paul demands that this duty to facilitate restoration be carried out by individuals who are spiritual. Such spiritual Christians are those who exhibit the fruits of the Spirit. These fruits of the Spirit are listed in Gal. 5:22-23a, namely, "love, joy, peace, patience, kindness, goodness, faithfulness, gentleness, self-control." The gentleness of which St. Paul speaks is a gentleness of strength. Jesus applied the word "gentle" to Himself when He said: "Take My yoke upon you, and learn from Me; for I am gentle and lowly in heart, and you will find rest for your souls" (Matt. 11:29).

Immediately after his directive to restore the person who has trespassed, St. Paul says: "Bear one another's burdens, and so fulfill the law of Christ" (Gal. 6:2). Since this injunction follows so immediately, many have concluded that one of the burdens Christians need to bear is having to confront those among us who have sinned.

Paul does not specify what types of sin qualify under the general heading of being "overtaken in any trespass." If one places the emphasis on the word "any," then it is perfectly appropriate to include the sin of neglecting the means of grace as a sin which needs to be gently called to the attention of the sinner. That gentle reminder can be done most effectively by the fellow Christian who depends upon the means of grace to maintain the ability to offer the word of admonition with gentleness and in a spirit of friendliness.

In Eph. 4:25—5:20 St. Paul offers a number of directives concerning the sanctified life which Christians are expected to lead. He makes clear how God's plan of salvation, which is described in some detail in the prior chapters, is to be applied in the lives of Christian people. Most of the actions listed by St. Paul encourage his readers not to commit various immoral acts. He recognized that even though the church exists in "light," there still is "darkness" both in the world that surrounds the church and even within Christians themselves, in their "old Adam." It is imperative that the darkness be identified and lighted by the grace of God.

Among the many "thou shalt nots" of Eph. 4:25—5:20 there are some important "thou shalts" which relate directly to the need to confront individuals who have become inactive. Eph. 4:32—5:2 reads: ". . . and be kind to one another, tenderhearted, forgiving one another, as God in Christ forgave you. Therefore be imitators of God, as beloved children. And walk in love, as Christ loved us and gave Himself up for us, a fragrant offering and sacrifice to God." Here we are urged to forgive fellow Christians. According to Paul, the ability to forgive is motivated by Christ's sweet-smelling sacrifice.

A second important "thou shalt" is presented in Eph. 5:18-20: "And do not get drunk with wine, for that is debauchery; but be filled with the Spirit, addressing one another in psalms and hymns and spiritual songs, singing and making melody to the Lord with all your heart, always and for everything giving thanks in the name of our Lord Jesus Christ to God the Father."

The only way for a Christian to carry out these directives is in concert with fellow Christians who have been motivated by the Holy Spirit.

Absence of interaction between fellow Christians makes it difficult if not impossible to maintain a fully developed Christian experience. Therefore inactivity must be identified and inactives must be assisted to become active once again. It is in the interaction with fellow Christians that one can speak and sing as Paul suggests.

In 2 Thess. 3:6-15 St. Paul indicates that "any brother" who is guilty of living in idleness should be avoided. He encourages faithful Christians to work as he had worked while he was in their midst. He writes: "If anyone refuses to obey what we say in this letter, note that man, and have nothing to do with him, that he may be ashamed. Do not look on him as an enemy, but warn him as a brother" (2 Thess. 3:14-15).

Paul directs the faithful at Thessalonica to (1) "mark well"[33] the person who did not respond to his directives, (2) avoid the person so noted so that he would be ashamed, and (3) tell the person the truth of God so that he can be restored to the fellowship. But even though the brother is to be confronted, he remains a brother and not an enemy. The desire is to win the brother.

It is important to recognize that Paul had addressed the issue of idleness in his first epistle (1 Thess. 5:14). Therefore when he returns to the issue of idleness in his second epistle he expresses himself even more strongly. He hereby recognizes that a person is no longer able to live for himself once he joins the fellowship of the church. Such a person is responsible for how people view God and how they see their brothers and sisters in Christ. The people outside the church judge the church on the basis of what church members do in public. Idleness created a negative view of the church of Christ in Thessalonica. Therefore the willfully idle person is to be disciplined.

This material from Second Thessalonians is less easily applied to discipline over against inactive members. However, this material is significant in that it is consistent with what we have already learned about the Biblical view of church discipline. Paul's approach always emphasizes *love as the motive* for approaching the brother or sister, and *restoration to fellowship* as the goal to be achieved.

In the Roman Empire during the last half of the first century the pressing issue for Christians was endurance in the faith versus apostasy: "The saying is sure: If we have died with Him, we shall also live with Him; if we endure, we shall also reign with Him; if we deny Him, He also will deny us; if we are faithless, He remains faithful—for He cannot deny Himself" (2 Tim. 2:11-13). This emphasis is also made in Heb. 10:26-39.

Thus the late New Testament literature exhorts the faithful to persevere (Heb. 12:1). Jesus is the model of perseverance (Heb. 12:2), while Esau is the example cited to demonstrate what happens to people who are not disciplined (Heb. 12:16-17). Jesus as a model is especially important, for suffering and persecution are going to happen in the lives of Christians (Heb. 12:3-11).

St. Paul's explanation to Timothy concerning how Hymenaeus and Alexander have been handled (1 Tim. 1:20), namely that Paul has "delivered [them] to Satan," must be recognized as being remedial, "that they may learn not to blaspheme." Paul's intention was to teach and discipline people so that they would be led to repentance.[34] As one author has written: "However stringent the process, the motive was mercy, and whenever ecclesiastical discipline has departed from this purpose of restoration, its harshness has proved a barrier to progress. But this is no reason for dispensing with discipline entirely, a failing which frequently characterizes our modern churches."[35]

Some people suggest that the concept of discipline in First and Second Timothy, Hebrews, First Peter, and Revelation is more penal in character than the concept of discipline described in the earlier New Testament materials. Particularly the theme of discipline as being comprised of suffering and perseverance is evident in the later documents.[36]

## Application of the Bible's Teachings on Church Discipline

It is important that people who have become inactive are not automatically assumed to be apostate. To conclude that someone is apostate demands more diagnostic information than merely the fact that the person has stopped attending church services and the functions of church auxiliaries. However, inactivity *may be* caused by apostasy. Therefore an analysis of a person's inactivity may produce the conclusion that the person has indeed become an apostate.

One of the major emphases of the Holy Scriptures and also of the Lutheran confessional writings is that the church is the community of God's people in which forgiveness of sin is expressed and lived out on a day-by-day basis. It is in and through the church that God proclaims and grants the forgiveness of sin. This emphasis on the forgiveness of sin assists God's people in placing church discipline in a helpful perspective. Church discipline is an aspect of the process by which the Law and the Gospel are properly employed to produce sanctified changes in the lives of God's people.

Although many may not realize it, church discipline can be described as one of the marks of the church. The Lutheran confessional writings designate the proclamation of God's Word and the faithful administration of the sacraments as marks of the church.[37] However, confession is also identified as a mark of the church in the Apology of the Augsburg Confession.[38]

Jesus stated very directly that the church has the responsibility to "loose" and to "bind" people's sins (Matt. 16:18-19; Matt. 18:15-20; John 20:21-23). "Loosing sins" is dependent on a confession of sin. That confession is immediately to be followed by absolution.

"Binding sins" is done to cause people to recognize their sinfulness, take stock of their alienation over against God, and demonstrate their lostness because of their refusal to repent and receive God's gift of grace expressed in forgiveness. Therefore the purpose of binding is to serve the cause of the Gospel. The hope of Christian people is that this preachment of Law will be a means to awaken the sleeping conscience of the sinner.

When such binding and loosing does not take place, the church is less than it ought to be. Jesus intended the church to exercise this power and responsibility on God's behalf.[39]

On the other hand, "One of the signs of a vital Christian community will be that the Word of God is voluntarily offered and received by all of its members, the Word that comforts and the Word that reproves. The Word of admonition and rebuke must be ventured where defection from God's Word in doctrine or life threatens the Christian fellowship."[40]

To assure a God-pleasing application of church discipline means that all congregations must study the Scriptures in order to discern, with the aid of the Holy Spirit, what the will of God is concerning the subject of church discipline. What is more, a lack of interest in the proper application of church discipline is at least partially motivated by the fact that the Word of God has not sufficiently been brought to bear on the lives of the members of the congregation. When the Word of God is studied, it becomes clear that discipline is done in order to promote mutual love and brotherhood in the congregation. It also becomes clear that the Word of God "is a Law-Gospel Word, a threat-promise Word, a judgment-mercy Word."[41]

When church discipline is ignored, the inference can be drawn that the church, and particularly God, cares little about the lives Christians lead. Such a message works at cross purposes with the message of the damning nature of sin which is proclaimed from the pulpit and taught in the classroom. When church discipline is applied, the church is practicing what it is preaching and teaching. God does not overlook or condescendingly ignore sinful activities. Therefore, without a consistent application of church discipline, confusion results among church members concerning the nature of God's will as proclaimed in His law.

When the law of God is both proclaimed and lived out through a systematic and responsible application of church discipline, then the message of the Gospel is sweet music to people's ears. Once the reality of God's judgment over against sin is taken to heart, then the message of God's forgiveness is a message of joy and peace.

It should also be noted that when the church does not practice what it preaches the church's proclamation can be judged by outsiders as hypocritical. The church that does not address the beam in its own eye has little credibility when talking about the speck in the eyes of those outside.

When Christian people speak the Gospel, the Holy Spirit uses this means of grace to move people from the rule of Satan to the rule of Christ. When that Gospel Word of forgiveness is offered, some people will receive all that God gives in that Word. They believe, and salvation is granted to them. Others, when confronted by the Gospel Word, perceive it as a stumbling block and an offense. When such a response is forthcoming, the church cannot apply the Word of forgiveness and mercy to the unbelieving person's life. Thus, when the Word of God is spoken and the hearers of that Word do not believe that their sins are forgiven and they reject the Gospel message, they are condemned to temporal and eternal punishment for their sins.

Some Christians excuse their inaction over against their brothers and sisters who are sinning with the rationalism that since they themselves are sinners they cannot confront a fellow sinner. Perhaps such people even cite Matt. 7:3-5, Jesus' words about the log and/or speck in people's eyes, as a prooftext to further legitimize their lack of action.

In light of the Biblical witness presented earlier in this chapter, those who are reluctant to employ church discipline need to contemplate the implications of such reluctance. To ignore the tears of a lost child in the supermarket, the difficulty of a blind person trying to cross a busy street, or the shouts for help from a person being attacked would be judged as loveless and irresponsible inaction. Yet when a brother or sister in Christ stumbles and falls into sin a different set of values seems to come into play. Under such circumstances many seem to think that the "correct" action to take is to legitimize inactivity by asserting acceptance, defending the rights of individuals to have different opinions and life-styles, expressing a superficial sentimental concept of love, and remonstrating about not wishing to be judgmental.

But when one evaluates these "correct" responses, one cannot help but note how far they have moved from the will of God and the mind of

Christ. To allow a Christian brother or sister to wander around in a world of sin, indifference, guilt, moral laxity, and separation from the means of grace is to abdicate one's responsibilities as a fellow Christian and to abandon that person to the power of sin, death, and the devil. Is there any more obvious example of lovelessness than this? Should we not react in moral outrage that such indifference is allowed to pass for sensitive Christianity?

Furthermore, it must be said that not only lack of discipline but also its perfunctory application dare not be equated with a ministry that emphasizes mutual love. This mutual love must be part of the very warp and woof of parish life. Mutual love takes seriously the need to confront erring brothers and sisters in Christ.

Dietrich Bonhoeffer noted: "Nothing can be more cruel than the tenderness that consigns another to his sin. Nothing can be more compassionate than the severe rebuke that calls a brother back from the path of sin."[42] Bonhoeffer also wrote: "When Christians live together, the time must inevitably come when in some crisis one person will have to declare God's Word and will to another. . . . The basis upon which Christians can speak to one another is that each one knows the other as a sinner, who, with all his human dignity, is lonely and lost if he is not given help."[43] Said another way, "Mutual care in the church means enduring the fact that each of its members is *simul justus et peccator*."[44]

Properly understood then, discipline is being carried out by God over against every Christian every day. Congregations are not composed of one group of people who are to discipline their fellow members and a second group which is to be disciplined. The more accurate view is that Christian people sometimes are used by God to assist in providing discipline to their fellow members while on other occasions they are the recipients of discipline.[45]

The previous paragraphs are properly understood when it is realized that just because a congregation has not excommunicated anyone for the past 10 years does not mean that church discipline is absent from that congregation. Church discipline at its best is the daily admonitions that brothers and sisters in Jesus Christ share with each other day in and day out. Church discipline at its best means that such careful and consistent admonition has taken place that there has been no need for excommunication.

Discipline in the Biblical sense is a positive word. It has been said that "Discipline is the continuing work of discipleship."[46] Therefore discipline and discipleship are closely associated with one another. Because of the link between discipline and discipleship and discipline and sanctification it is also proper to say that "True discipline is preventive discipline."[47] Preventive discipline means helping our fellow members live the sanctified life to such an extent that sin does not express itself in manifest ways. Discipline makes sense if we recognize that the church is not sent to the world to make converts but to make disciples.

Discipline in the New Testament assumes that there is a standard by which the Christian lives of people are to be measured. That standard is the will of God.[48] As one author has written: "To be united to Christ means to be identified with Christ's attitude to sin. It means seeing sin with Jesus' eyes, and opposing it with something of the same passion with which Jesus at Calvary opposed it. It means an assent of the whole man to the divine judgment proclaimed upon sin at the cross. It means, as the writer to the Hebrews says, 'resistance unto blood.' It means as Paul put it tersely, 'death.'"[49]

The words of the quotation above make it clear that discipline serves as a corrective to the "cheap grace" concept which is so much a part of modern church life and proclamation.[50] Therefore discipline means that judgment must be passed, not in the penal sense but in the pastoral sense of the word.

In the pastoral sense the word "discipline" means "such uses of discipline as are designed to comfort, strengthen and inspire the weakling; by the latter [penal sense] such usages as have for their purposes to cut off the Church from the world by cutting off the weakling from the Church."[51]

Coiner has written: "The church must not attempt to separate all sinners from the godly, in the sense of purging itself, but rather must seek to sanctify the sinners through the Gospel."[52]

The pastoral use of discipline does not imply self-righteousness, while self-righteousness is clearly an aspect of penal discipline (cf. Matt. 7:1-5; also Matt. 7:15-27).

Application of church discipline must also be informed by the continuing guidance of the Holy Spirit. And because of Christ's promise, the truth can be affirmed that as the church carries out its responsibility to "loose" and to "bind" it can count on the presence and guidance of the Holy Spirit (John 14:26; 16:12-14; 20:22-23). Church discipline must focus on the cross because that event provides the means by which all Christians, including erring Christians, are forgiven. But without the abiding presence and guidance of the Holy Spirit it would be impossible for the church to co-judge with God. Without the guidance of the Holy Spirit it is impossible for Christ's body to discern what is the will of God. Without the Holy Spirit's guidance the church will not have the courage to exercise church discipline. Jesus realized this, and that is why He promised His disciples and His people today the gift of the Holy Spirit.

Christian congregations that are serious about church discipline must also be serious about the discipline imposed by other Christian churches. If such discipline culminates in excommunication, that action is excommunication from the church of Jesus Christ. It is not simply excommunication from a given local congregation. When Christian congregations accept as new members individuals who were excommunicated by other congregations, they had better be completely convinced that the individuals have repented of their sins and have received forgiveness for those sins or that the excommunication was a miscarriage of justice because of a faulty application of God's law or an inappropriate unwillingness on the part of the membership of the former congregation to proclaim absolution to penitent sinners.

If congregations do not honor the proper disciplinary actions of other congregations, they are guilty of offering cheap grace, and they are making a mockery of Christ's wishes concerning what sins are to be "loosed" and what sins are to be "bound."

The Bible clearly teaches that church discipline is an important component of the church's life. When discipline is not applied, the church is weakened. Without discipline the church is weakened because its message is blunted and its members are allowed to become spiritually flabby. Church discipline needs to be applied whenever Christians stray from the path God has laid out for His people. Wandering from God includes absenting oneself from the means of grace, from fellowship, from the breaking of bread, and from corporate prayer.

Church discipline is a loving act, because it has as its goal the reclaiming of the brother or sister in Christ. Application of church discipline means that Christians value the erring person and care enough to make the effort to assist in the restoration of one who is overcome by sin. It is the absence rather than the presence of church discipline which is lacking in Christian love. Without discipline the church is less than it ought to be, for it has ignored its responsibility to exercise mutual care and love.

# Chapter 5

# Preparing to Minister to Inactives

The preceding chapters have presented information concerning factors that seem to produce inactivity, steps that can be taken to enhance retention of members, issues that must be considered when inactives are ministered to, and theological issues and practical considerations that must be addressed as congregations employ church discipline. The purpose of this chapter is to suggest some critical questions that the leaders of congregations need to answer prior to initiating a concerted effort to minister to inactive members.

Before a congregation or its leaders decide to initiate, restructure, or redirect the congregation's ministry to inactives, there are a number of crucial questions that need to be asked and answered. Some of those questions are implied or expressed in the discussion that follows. The material is offered as illustrative, and it is not meant to be exhaustive. Congregations may have to add to or delete from the list depending on their unique situation.

## What Data Needs to Be Gathered?

It seems rather obvious that it is imperative to determine the number of inactive members a congregation has before plans are developed to minister to them. In order to make such an analysis, the term "inactive" has to be defined. To do this, decisions must be made about whether individuals such as those who have moved from the community, are away from home attending college, or are serving in the military will be included in the count.

The purpose of asking these questions is to determine the number of inactive people in the congregation who need to be recipients of the congregation's visitation ministry and who are reasonably available for such ministry. At the same time asking these questions helps to determine what strategies need to be developed in order to minister to those who are not living in close enough proximity to the church or the community to warrant including them among the ones to be visited.

## Whose Ministry Is It?

Unless Christian people and Christian congregations accept the responsibility they have for individuals who have become inactive, many of those inactive members will remain inactive. However, when a task is everybody's, it very frequently becomes nobody's. In a very real sense, concern about fellow Christians who have become inactive ought to be the responsibility of every Christian, yet perhaps not every Christian is gifted with the skills and attitudes necessary to carry out such a ministry.

In the material that follows it is assumed that because of their Christian concern congregations will identify those individuals in their midst who are particularly gifted for this work.

The constitutions of many congregations list ministry to inactive members as one of the duties of the members of the board of elders. Other constitutions may place this responsibility with a board of deacons, board of evangelism, or some other group.

There are probably many good reasons to continue to identify the ministry to inactives as the responsibility of the board(s) designated in a congregation's constitution. However, it must also be recognized that just because individuals are elected to serve on such boards does not mean they have the gifts of faith, temperament, ability to listen, etc., that are helpful, if not prerequisite, characteristics of "successful" visitors of inactive members.

It is imperative that the leaders of a congregation give careful thought to who should be responsible for making the visits on inactive members.

Specific characteristics and attitudes which seem helpful for the visitors to possess will become more explicit as this chapter and the following one are read and understood. Therefore it is important that these chapters be worked through as carefully as possible before identifying and recruiting a group of callers. In general it can be said that the five most important characteristics for callers to possess are: (1) love for brothers and sisters in Jesus Christ, (2) nonjudgmental attitude, (3) patience, (4) ability to listen empathetically, and (5) commitment to Jesus Christ.

## How Does the Congregation Plan to Respond to Reasons Inactives Cite for Being Inactive?

It is important that the reader remember the complexities which arise as congregations and individuals attempt to minister to inactives. Since inactives feel they have good reasons to be inactive, congregations have to face the fact that they may need to make some changes and adjustments in order to correct the "problems" that are identified by the inactive members.

Congregational leaders who want to take seriously a comprehensive ministry to inactive members will at least need to lay out the procedures for how the recommended adjustments will be identified, evaluated, planned, and carried out. Even better, some changes need to be made prior to initiating any visitation of inactive members. Congregational leaders can and ought to take some measures to (1) strengthen the congregation's ministry to families, (2) enrich the worship experience, (3) assimilate new members, (4) provide a dynamic youth program, etc., even aside from their concern about ministry to inactive members. When this concern is added, they will be even more highly motivated to address the "weaknesses" or "inadequacies" in the congregation's ministry.

These cautions suggest that an effective ministry to inactives may be frustrated because problems and concerns which inactives identify in the congregation need to be heeded; yet it is to misuse them if they become excuses to explain why congregations cannot initiate or carry out such a ministry. Raising cautions is prudent behavior when it causes people to "count the cost before building the tower," but cautions which become rationalizations are paralyzing.

Simply said, an effective program of ministry to inactive members will in all likelihood cause a ripple effect which will finally touch and perhaps modify in some way much of what a congregation is and does. Some modifications will be subtle and of little consequence for anyone except those inactives who have had their concerns addressed, while others may need to be much more substantive if the inactive members' objections are going to be satisfied. The congregation will have to decide if it is willing to make such substantive changes. Perhaps it will not be willing in light of the witness of Scripture, or it may be that in matters of adiaphora the congregation simply chooses not to make adjustments.

It would be very helpful to develop mutually acceptable procedures by which the cadre of visitors could share concerns, offer suggestions, raise questions, etc., with members of the boards and committees of the congregation and with its professional staff.

## Should the Congregation Consider Taking Action to Correct Inadequacies in Its Ministry Prior to Beginning Work with Inactive Members?

It might be a very helpful exercise for the leaders of the congregation to complete a copy of the questionnaire which is included among the activities for Session 6, in the sixth chapter of this book. Honest responses may produce data which will help give directions for adjustments that need to be made. In one sense the questionnaire can serve as a means to make a needs analysis. It may be wise for the leaders of the congregation to add to the questionnaire other questions which reflect the unique problems, concerns, or ministry programs of the congregation.

## Summary

One purpose of the questions and discussion above is to emphasize how very important it is for the leaders of a congregation to prepare it for the variety of implications that could arise because of a ministry to inactives. At the same time it is also important to recognize that if the proper preparations are not made to respond to the unmet needs of inactive members it will greatly magnify the difficulties faced by the visitors and perhaps preclude the possibility of activating many of the inactive members. Therefore if a congregation's choice is to select, train, and send out visitors without making the necessary preparations to assist the callers and respond to the information they gather, that congregation is being shortsighted, perhaps even irresponsible.

Chapter 6

# A Suggested Plan
# to Train Lay Visitors
# to Carry Out a Ministry
# of Visitation

There are a number of important preliminary steps that must be taken before a group of people is gathered to be trained to carry out a ministry to inactive members of the congregation.

It is imperative that the following steps have been taken before a group of people is recruited to participate in the training program outlined in this chapter.

1. The responsible board(s) or committee(s) (i.e., board of elders, board of evangelism, church council or voter's assembly) have made certain that all the planning questions raised in chapter 5 have been answered and proper procedures established.

2. A group facilitator has been selected to lead the training sessions that follow.

3. All the participants have been given a copy of this book, and they have read the Introduction and the first five chapters.

4. All the participants have made a commitment to take part in the entire training process and have agreed to serve as visitors on inactive members of the congregation.

The lesson plans for the 16 sessions that follow have been designed to take a maximum of one-and-a-half hours each. A suggested time schedule has been included. The person serving as group facilitator should use information about the members of the group, the parish, etc., to modify the designs of the lesson plans to assure that the process will be as useful as possible.

The group leader should also make certain that the meeting place is as conducive as possible to assure maximum participation by group members. Discussion happens best when people are seated in circles, and when they are given time to work with ideas in small groups. Conversations while eating snacks and drinking hot or cold beverages served at breaks or after the study sessions can provide another opportunity for additional fellowship and continued conversation among group members.

The group facilitator will frustrate the process inherent in these lesson plans if he feels the need to lecture. If visitors are going to be enabled to feel as comfortable as possible about making calls on inactive members, those visitors must have had the experience of listening and responding to one another in the "safe" setting of the group. This process of listening and responding to one another builds their confidence in themselves and their teammates. This confidence and competence is not gained as effectively by merely listening to a group leader speak.

## Session 1

I. Introduction

You have come together at this time and place to initiate a learning process which has been designed to help you become a more effective witness for God. The effective witness you will make has as its intended audience fellow members of your congregation who have dropped out of parish life. The learning sessions which you will experience have been written with the assumption that you have read the Introduction and chapters 1—4 of this book.

II. Objectives

At the conclusion of this session the participants will be able to: (1) identify one another by name; (2) provide an overview of the training experience they will undergo; (3) be conscious of their own feelings about the congregation of which they are members; (4) be conscious of their own feelings about inactive members of their congregation; (5) express their expectations of the learning experience; (6) express any fears or apprehensions they may have concerning the learning process; (7) express any fears or apprehensions they may have concerning being part of the congregation's ministry to inactive people; and (8) commit themselves to participation in the entirety of the learning process outlined on the remaining pages of this book.

III. Supplies needed

Newsprint/blackboard, magic markers/chalk, masking tape/thumb tacks, sheets of paper, pens/pencils, items for the devotion, 4 x 6 index cards, and an easel.

IV. Devotion

A short devotion should be prepared and led by the group facilitator at this initial meeting. Henceforth members of the group may need to be encouraged or will want to lead the devotion which begins each session.

These devotions could include reading pertinent Scriptural material, hymns, litanies, prayers, testimonies, and group sharing.

Devotional thoughts shared should not offer "answers" to questions or "resolutions" to problems and issues that will be addressed later in the session.

V. Activities

In many small and relatively stable congregations the learning of participants' names may not be necessary because people have known each other for years. However, in most urban and suburban congregations members do not necessarily know one another. In order for the processes that have been built into this experience to work, it is imperative that people know each other. It may be helpful for the participants to wear a name tag to the first few meetings.

A. Each person is to take a 4 x 6 index card and a magic marker. Ask each person to write his/her first name on the center of the card.

1. In the upper left corner write a word or short phrase or draw a picture which describes or expresses your view of yourself.

2. In the upper right corner write a word or short phrase or draw a picture which describes or expresses your relationship to the congregation of which you are a member.

3. In the lower left corner write a word or short phrase or draw a picture which describes or expresses your feelings about inactive members of your congregation.

4. In the lower right corner write a word or short phrase or draw a picture which describes or expresses the major personal quality or characteristic which you have to offer to your congregation's ministry to inactive members. (Allow 5 to 10 minutes for this activity.)

B. After you have all completed your cards, share with one another your name and the words or phrases or pictures you have written or drawn on your cards. Make sure that each of you has ample time to say all you want to say. Also, feel free to ask questions of clarification if you do not understand what your fellow participant has said. (Allow 10 to 15 minutes for this activity.)

C. After you have shared the information, make two loops of masking tape, attach a portion of the loops to the back side of the 4 x 6 card, and use the rest of the loops to tape the card to your shirt or blouse. These cards will serve as your name tags.

D. You undoubtedly have some expectations of this training experience which is designed to make you an effective ambassador for Jesus Christ to inactive members of your congregation. Such expectations need to be recognized at this time and, it is hoped, addressed systematically in the sessions that follow.

1. On a piece of paper provided to you develop a list of your individual expectations of this training event. Be as specific as possible. Work alone developing your list. (Allow 5 minutes for this activity.)

2. Now in diads of two persons share your expectations with one another. Note similarities and differences in each of your lists. Discuss with one another those items on your lists which you feel comfortable discussing. (Allow 10 minutes for this activity.)

3. Now as a diad meet with another diad. Share your lists with one another. Note the expectations you have in common and rank the expectations into three categories.

a. Category #1-This should include all expectations which are very important, those you feel must be met in order for the experience to be of benefit to you.

b. Category #2-This should include all expectations which are somewhat important, those you feel would be helpful if met but are not an absolute necessity.

c. Category #3-This should include items which would be nice fringe benefits but are not necessary for you to have or experience for you to serve as an ambassador of Jesus Christ to inactive members of your congregation.

4. Write all the expectations in Category #1 on a single sheet of newsprint and all the expectations in Category #2 on a second sheet of newsprint. If you have time, write all of the items in Category #3 on a third sheet of newsprint. Be sure to label each sheet appropriately. (Allow 20 minutes for this activity.)

5. Discuss with one another any fears and apprehensions you may have about being involved in a ministry to inactive members. Share

whatever feelings you are comfortable sharing. (Allow 10 minutes for this activity.)

6. Form one large group. In order for the group facilitator to help the group to work through the expectations and fears of its members, that facilitator needs to have become familiar with the remaining pages of this book to assure acquaintance with the content and processes that the group will experience in the later training sessions. Share with one another your composite lists. As each group shares its list, offer any words of explanation that are necessary. (Allow 10 to 15 minutes for this activity.)

VI. Summary

The group facilitator should quickly remind the participants of all the things they have done during the 90 minutes they have spent together. This is an important step in the process. The summary period should not be skipped. Highlight in particular the information developed in V., D. above. Encourage the participants to continue to think and pray about the items discussed at this first session.

VII. Assignment

Spend some time during the days between now and the second meeting of the group in reading, studying, meditating on, and praying about Luke 15.

VIII. Closing Devotion

Perhaps the closing devotion could include a prayer, the singing of a stanza or two of a hymn, and the benediction.


# Session 2

I. Introduction

As Christian people you believe that the benefits you receive from learning together will be increased as you turn to God's Word for insight and direction. It is God's Word that gives you grace, power, inspiration, commitment, assistance, and direction. Therefore the major input in session 2 is contained in the 15th chapter of the Gospel According to St. Luke. The three parables that are recorded in Luke 15 have much to say to Christian people about the nature of God the Father, His concern that all people should be saved, and the unhelpful attitudes and practices held and carried out by "religious people." These attitudes of "religious people" are often diametrically opposed to the will and plan God has for His people who are outside of or who are drifting away from His kingdom.

II. Objectives

At the conclusion of this session the participants will be able to: (1) interpret the three parables of Jesus which are recorded in Luke 15; (2) list specific applications of the parables to the life of their congregation; (3) identify specific correlations between the attitudes of the Pharisees, scribes, and the older brother and their own attitudes toward people who are lost, particularly those in danger because they have dropped out of congregational life; (4) list ways in which the power of the Gospel message may be applied to help "active members" develop attitudes which are more in conformity to the will of God; and (5) begin to formulate a strategy for confronting inactive people which takes seriously the love and acceptance of God the Father, who wishes to receive joyfully those who have been lost.

III. Supplies needed

Bibles, sheets of paper, newsprint, magic markers, pens/pencils, masking tape/thumb tacks, and an easel.

IV. Devotion

V. Activities

A. Read Luke 15 in its entirety. You may read it aloud as a group or quietly to yourselves. As you read note:

1. the nature of the incident which originally caused Jesus to tell the parables;

2. the point of comparison in each parable; (Each parable makes a chief point, called the point of comparison.)

3. how God the Father is depicted in the parables;

4. the role the elder brother plays in the third parable; (Does the older brother represent the scribes and Pharisees? Does the older brother represent "religious people" who live in the modern era?)

5. what the Gospel message has to say to inactive members;

6. what the Gospel message has to say to active members; and

7. what clues the parables provide concerning conducting a ministry directed to inactive members. (Allow 10 to 15 minutes for this activity.)

B. On sheets of paper provided, the participants are to write the following three sentence stems.

1. What I believe these parables of Jesus are saying to me as a Christian person is . . .

2. What I believe these parables of Jesus are saying to the active members of our congregation is . . .

3. What I believe these parables of Jesus are saying about inactive members of our congregation is . . .

97

C. Complete these sentence stems with as many alternate endings as possible. (Allow at least 10 minutes for this activity.)

D. If the group is six people or larger, form into groups of three people each. Please share with one another in your small groups as many of the phrases you wrote to complete the sentence stems as you are comfortable sharing. (Allow at least 15 minutes for this activity.)

1. Each person should share what he/she has written in response to the first sentence stem. Please discuss any statements which anyone in the group feels comfortable discussing.

2. Note ideas shared which you did not include on your own list.

3. Write on newsprint with magic marker or on a piece of paper with pen or pencil *all* the responses of the members of the group.

E. You have now developed one or more lists of responses to the three sentence stems. If there is more than one group, share the content of each group's list with the members of the other groups. Take the necessary time to allow questions of clarification to be raised and answered. (Allow at least 10 minutes for this activity.)

F. Take the necessary time to discuss the answers to the following questions in your small groups. Make notes of the major ideas that group members offer during the discussion. "If we take seriously what God the Spirit is saying to us in Luke 15 . . ." (Do not be satisfied with superficial comments. Try to capture the richness of content of these three parables. Allow your creativity, faith, and commitment to express themselves.)

1. what attitudes will have to be changed in my heart and mind?

2. what attitudes will have to change in the hearts and minds of the members of our congregation?

3. what changes will have to be made in our congregation's approach to ministering to inactive members? (Allow at least 10 minutes for this activity.)

G. After the small-group discussion, the entire group should develop a composite list of responses to these three questions. Write the responses on newsprint. Keep the newsprint so that it can be referred to at the next meeting of the group. (Allow 10 minutes for this activity.)

VI. Summary

The group facilitator should quickly remind the participants of all the things they have done during the 90 minutes they have spent together. Particularly highlight the data generated in V., F. and recorded in V., G. above. These data provide an ongoing working agenda for the group. Encourage the participants to continue to reflect on Luke 15 in the days ahead.

VII. Assignment

Reread Chapter IV of this book prior to the next meeting of the group.

VIII. Closing Devotion

## Session 3

I. Introduction

Luke 15 is very important in shaping how Christian people think and feel about individuals who have drifted from the faith. However, Luke 15 is not the only section of Scripture which is suitable for answering questions about how Christians need to respond to individuals who are in danger of losing or have lost the faith. Other important thoughts from God have been identified and highlighted in chapter 4 of this book. In this session the participants will have the opportunity to encounter some of these additional thoughts from God.

II. Objectives

At the conclusion of this learning experience the participants will be able to: (1) refine the list of responses to the three questions the group developed and put on newsprint in session 2; (2) share specific feelings they have about the subject of church discipline; (3) apply the words of Matthew 18 to their lives; (4) apply the concept that toleration of sinful behavior within a local congregation infects the entire congregation with sin; (5) discuss the implications of the judgment which says that "the incestuous young man of 1 Corinthians 5 cannot be the same man Paul refers to in 2 Cor. 2:5-11 because incest is such a terrible sin Paul would not have urged the Corinthians to take him back."

III. Supplies needed

Newsprint sheets from session 2, Bibles, paper, pens/pencils, newsprint and magic markers, blackboard and chalk, and an easel.

IV. Devotion

V. Activities

A. The group facilitator should hang up the newsprint sheets developed by the participants during session 2 so that all can see what is written on the sheets.

B. The group facilitator may read aloud the content of the sheets to remind the participants what they had decided to include on the sheets. (Allow up to 5 minutes for these activities.)

C. Each participant should now take a blank piece of paper and a pen or pencil.

1. Please listen carefully to all the directions.

2. In just a moment I am going to give you two words.

3. As soon as I give you the words I want all of you to write on your sheet of paper every word or phrase that comes to mind as a result of your hearing the words.

4. The process you are doing might be called "word associating" or "free associating."

5. Once again, write down any word or phrase that comes to mind after hearing the words.

6. The words I want you to concentrate on are "church discipline." (Allow 3 minutes for this activity.)

D. Look at all the words or phrases on your sheet of paper.

1. Place a + (plus sign) beside each word or phrase which seems to carry a positive loading or connotation for you.

2. Place a - (minus sign) beside each word or phrase which seems to carry a negative loading or connotation for you. (Allow 2 minutes for this activity.)

E. How many of you had more positively loaded words or phrases than negatively loaded ones?

F. How many of you had more negatively loaded words or phrases than positively loaded ones?

G. Talk about the possible reasons why negatively loaded words or phrases come to mind when you hear the words "church discipline."

1. Entitle a sheet of newsprint "Causes of Negative Loading."

2. Write on newsprint the reasons that are suggested.

3. Attempt to summarize the suggestions in not more than three or four words.

4. Suggest how this list might have been different if this activity had been done prior to your having read chapter 4 of this book. (Allow 10 to 15 minutes for this activity.)

H. Divide the larger group into groups of four individuals each.

1. Read through all of Matthew 18. You may do this aloud or silently.

2. In your group discuss whether Matthew 18 helps to address or call into question any of the causes suggested as to why the words "church discipline" elicited negative feelings.

3. Discuss any confusion any participants might feel between the need to confront evil and the desire to save the sinner. (Allow at least 25 minutes for this activity.)

I. Remain in your small groups of four each.

1. Turn to 1 Corinthians 5.

2. In 1 Corinthians 5 Paul argues that tolerating immorality in the life

of the church infects the entire congregation with that immorality.

3. Discuss with one another the specific implications this concept has for your congregation.

4. Should the behavior of withdrawing from the life of a Christian congregation be equated with immorality? (Gal. 6:1) If so, how would you propose to apply Gal. 6:6-8 to your congregation? (Allow 15 minutes for this activity.)

J. Biblical scholars since the time of the church father Tertullian have said that the man identified by St. Paul in 2 Cor. 2:5-11 cannot be the same man Paul condemned in 1 Corinthians 5. The major reason proposed by many interpreters in holding this view is that they cannot accept the thought that Paul could counsel granting forgiveness, even if the incestuous man was penitent because of his gross sin.

1. Discuss with one another your reactions to this contention. Do you agree or disagree? Why?

2. What are the implications for your life and the lives of all sinners if you agree? if you disagree? (Allow 15 minutes for this activity.)

K. The group facilitator needs to call the entire group together again and ask:

1. "Are there any new thoughts that need to be added to the lists of ideas on the sheets prepared during Session 2?"

a. What attitudes will have to be changed in my heart and mind?

b. What attitudes will have to change in the hearts and minds of the leaders of our congregation?

c. What changes will have to be made in our congregation's approach to inactive members?

2. Add any items the participants suggest. (Allow up to 10 minutes for this activity.)

3. Reflect on the items listed on the newsprint sheet in answer to the question, "What attitudes will have to change in my heart and mind?" Ask yourself if any changes have happened already as a result of your study in this group. What changes have come about? How do you feel about those changes? (Allow 2 minutes for this activity.)

L. If any of you feel comfortable sharing any of the changes in attitude you perceive in yourself, do so at this time. (Allow up to 5 minutes for this activity.)

VI. Summary

VII. Assignment
   Reread chapter 3 of this book.

VIII. Closing Devotion

# Session 4

I. Introduction

Among the emphases of chapter 3 of this book is the contention that individuals who have dropped out of the life of a local congregation will be reactivated most successfully if they experience the genuine ministry of being listened to and cared about by individuals who are active in their former congregation.

Since the active members of a congregation also have personal agendas which very often conflict with the personal agendas of the dropouts, it is difficult for active members to function automatically as helpful listeners. Therefore it is necessary for active members to develop the necessary attitudes and skills to enable them to serve helpfully in this important ministry.

II. Objectives

At the conclusion of this learning experience the participants will be able to: (1) list behaviors which help people listen to others; (2) discuss the effects that listeners' attitudes have on their listening behaviors; (3) identify personal attitudes towards inactives that have changed or are in the process of changing; (4) suggest ways of dealing with feelings of inadequacy when making calls on inactive members; and (5) recognize specific listening behaviors when they are evidenced.

III. Supplies needed

Paper, pens/pencils, newsprint/blackboard, magic markers/chalk, masking tape/thumb tacks, and an easel.

IV. Devotion

V. Activities

A. Take the next two minutes to reflect on some of your personal experiences when you were trying to communicate to someone else things that were important to you.

1. What behaviors, on the part of the persons listening to you, helped you to feel that your concerns were being heard?

2. You may want to jot down some of your memories on a piece of paper as they occur to you. (Allow 2 minutes for this activity.)

B. Develop a list of effective listening behaviors which the group participants recall.

1. Write these behaviors on pieces of newsprint or on a blackboard.

2. Entitle the list "Behaviors which help people listen include . . ." (Allow up to 10 minutes for this activity.)

C. Divide the total group into small groups of three individuals each. Give them the following directions.

1. You have just developed a list of behaviors which are helpful in listening effectively.

2. Discuss with one another the implications you think these behaviors have for you as you visit with inactive people in your congregation.

3. Do you think some behaviors will be more difficult to exhibit than others? Which ones? Why? (Allow up to 15 minutes for this activity.)

D. Listening effectively is certainly assisted by employing helpful behaviors. However, behaviors are heavily influenced by the attitudes of the people who are trying to listen.

1. Turn to page 52 of this book.

2. Note there the commonly held attitudes of many active and inactive members of Christian congregations.

3. Do some personal reflection. Be as honest as you can with yourself. How similar are your attitudes to those of many active members toward the inactive as shown on the chart? (Allow 5 minutes for this activity.)

4. Talk with the members of your small group. Discuss with one another the following questions:

a. How much are my attitudes like the attitudes of typical active members?

b. How will my attitudes affect my ability to listen?

c. What do I need to do to change attitudes of mine that could cause me to be a less effective listener?

d. How do Luke 15, Matthew 18, 1 Corinthians 5, 2 Cor 2:5-11, and other passages we have discussed assist me in changing my unhelpful attitudes? (Allow up to 20 minutes for this activity.)

E. By this time in the process of reflecting upon and discussing listening behaviors and attitudes which affect listening behaviors, participants should have developed a significant body of important concerns, considerations, and data.

F. Turn to pages 57—59 of this book and quickly reread the material there. (Allow 5 minutes for this activity.)

G. You now need to return from your small groups to re-form the large group.

1. In your small groups you have been discussing your concerns about your own listening behaviors and the effects your attitudes about inactive fellow members might have on those behaviors.

2. During these next minutes you will be given an opportunity to talk

with others in the total group about concerns you have or questions with which you need help.

3. You may find the following questions helpful in stimulating your discussion, but do not feel limited to these suggested questions. Feel free to ask others in the group to respond to any concerns or questions you might have.

a. In order to maximize the learning in this setting, the total group, assuming it is not larger than 12 to 20, should be divided equally. If the group is larger than 20, divide it into equal groups of 6 to 10 members each. There needs to be an even number of groups.

b. Seat one group in a circle.

c. The seated group is to discuss the three questions that follow.

d. Ask the members of the second group to stand behind the chairs of the seated group.

e. Those standing are to remain quiet and not participate in the conversation.

f. The group members who are standing are assigned to watch the body language (facial expressions, posture, etc.) of the person seated across from them.

g. Make mental notes of all that you observe.

h. After 15 minutes have the groups switch roles.

i. Questions

1) Am I feeling overwhelmed by what I perceive is being expected of me as I try to listen effectively to inactive members of our congregation?

2) Do I feel the need for additional assistance in helping me to become a more effective listener? What type(s) of assistance do I need?

3) Do I feel any resentment or defensiveness because of the implicit labeling that may occur when I compare myself to the attitudes of many active members toward the inactive as shown on the chart? (Allow up to 30 minutes for this activity.)

H. What did you learn about listening or what truths about listening were reconfirmed by watching someone else listen?

1. Share what you observed.

2. Do not emphasize what individual people did. Emphasize behaviors observed. (Allow 10 to 15 minutes for this activity.)

VI. Summary

VII. Assignment

Try to stay "in touch" with your listening behaviors from the time of this meeting to the time of the next meeting of the group.

Reread chapter 3.

VIII. Closing Devotion

## Session 5

I. Introduction

During session 4 the group participants were reminded of some principles concerning effective listening and were encouraged to think about how those principles could be used as they make their visits in the homes of inactive members. The activities proposed for this session build on the concepts and ideas shared during session 4.

II. Objectives

At the conclusion of this learning experience the participants will be able to: (1) repeat key concepts concerning principles of effective listening that were shared in session 4; (2) provide answers for six questions which seek to encourage the participants to develop helpful responses to the attitudes, behaviors, questions, and comments of inactive members; and (3) develop skill in differentiating between statements which (a) describe what a person has seen, heard, touched, tasted, or smelled, (b) present what a person thinks, believes, or assumes, (c) state what a person feels, (d) express what a person *plans* on doing, and (e) set forth what a person has done, is doing, or will do.[1]

III. Supplies needed

This book, newsprint/blackboard, magic markers/chalk, masking tape/thumb tacks, and an easel.

IV. Devotion

V. Activities

A. Begin the session with all participants in a large group.

1. During our last session we talked about how to listen effectively.

2. Please help me list some of the most important concepts we discussed.

3. I am asking you to do this in order to help you remember the concepts and to set the context for this week's activities. (Allow up to 10 minutes for this activity.)

B. Effective communication is obviously dependent not only on the person who listens but also on the person who is speaking. You were asked to review chapter 3 of this book prior to this session. We are particularly interested in noting the behaviors and attitudes you might confront as you make your visits on inactive members.

C. Divide the group into small groups of four persons each.

1. Below are listed six questions.

2. Each small group will be given three to five minutes to suggest possible answers to question #1.

3. After the three to five minutes have elapsed, each group is to share its most helpful ideas with the members of the other groups. Eight to ten minutes should be provided for this sharing time.

4. After the eight to ten minutes have elapsed, the small groups are allotted three to five minutes to suggest answers for question #2.

5. This three- to five-minute discussion is to be followed by the eight- to ten-minute discussion of possible answers by the entire group.

6. This process of alternation continues until all six questions have been addressed.

D. Turn to page 52 of chapter 3.

1. Note the typical attitudes that many inactives possess about themselves and about active church members.

2. Respond to question #1. "How do you think you will respond to inactive fellow church members who exhibit the typical attitudes suggested in the chart on page 52?"

E. Return to page 52 of chapter 3.

1. Note the typical attitudes that many active members possess about themselves and about inactive members.

2. Respond to question #2. "Do you believe that you will find it difficult to remain objective and nondefensive as you listen to the excuses and real reasons that people say are causing them to be inactive?"

F. Turn to pages 56—57 in chapter 3.

1. Note the content of assumption #5 and the explanation of that assumption.

2. Respond to question #3. "How do you need to prepare yourself to respond to the excuses which will probably be expressed prior to the reason(s) for the inactivity of the individual(s) you are visiting?"

G. Respond to question #4. "How will you want to handle excuses or reasons which place blame on fellow members, church leaders, congregational practices, and the professional minister(s) of the congregation?"

H. Turn to pages 58—59 of chapter 3.

1. Note the content of assumption #8 and the explanation of that assumption.

2. Respond to question #5. "What techniques could you employ to help the individual(s) you are visiting to express the real causes for their inactivity as effectively and quickly as possible?"

I. Respond to question #6. "Are there any additional questions you have which are not reflected in the questions above?" (Allow a total of not more than 60 minutes for this activity.)

J. When people talk with one another, their statements can be identified as being representative of one of five kinds or types of statements, namely those which:

1. describe what a person has seen, heard, touched, tasted, or smelled;
2. present what a person thinks, believes, or assumes;
3. state what a person feels;
4. express what a person *intends* to do;
5. set forth what a person has done, is doing, or will do.

K. Below is a conversation. After each sentence of the conversation is a blank. After reading each statement, select which of the five kinds or types of statements listed above best describes its content. Please note that the conversation reflects that this is the fourth visit the visitor has made on the inactive member. "V" stands for visitor, while "I" represents the inactive member.

V: George, when I went home after our last conversation, I could not help but think you were not sharing with me all that bothers you. _____

I: I believe I have been honest with you. _____

V: I am not saying that you have not been honest. _____ I am merely sharing a feeling I have. _____ I cannot help but have the impression that you have not shared your major reason for becoming inactive. _____

I: I am feeling some pressure from you. _____ I am not sure I like that feeling. _____

V: I am sorry that I cause you to feel pressure. _____ I do not want to pressure you. _____ However, I care about you. _____ Because I care I want to try to assist you in whatever way I can. _____

I: You cannot help me. _____

V: Perhaps you are right, but I sure want to try. _____

I: It is too late to help me. _____

V: Once again, you may be right, but I would like to try. _____

I. I needed help nine years ago. _____ No one came then. _____ I was not important enough to get the attention I needed then. _____

V: What happened nine years ago? _____ I am sorry, but I do not know what happened nine years ago. _____

I: My first wife died. _____ The preacher came to talk with me briefly the day before the funeral. _____ He buried her, but he did not even come to the reception in the church basement after the funeral. _____ I sent him a $50 check for conducting the funeral. _____ He never called on me again. _____ Here I was. _____ All my relatives left to return to their homes. _____ I was left alone to grieve, to sort and give away her clothes. _____ It was awful. _____ I felt abandoned. _____ When I did not hear from the preacher for six weeks after the funeral, I vowed never to go back to church again. _____ What a bunch of hypocrites. _____ The preacher is the worst hypocrite of all. _____ All his words about caring for people and he does not even practice what he preaches by visiting with people who grieve. _____

V: That is a tragic story, George. _____ I am very sorry that everyone at church let you down at such a lonely time in your life. _____ I ask that you forgive us, George. _____ Also, I ask that you consider what you are doing to yourself. _____ I believe you are actually punishing yourself even though your goal is to punish the church. _____

I: What do you mean by that last statement? _____

ETC.

L.  After you have finished placing the numbers in the blanks, discuss with one another in the total group the following questions.

1. Was it difficult to identify what type of statement each statement was?

2. How does recognizing the type of statement being made help you to understand what the speaker is trying to say?

3. How can this process of being conscious of types of statements in everyday conversation be of assistance to you as you listen to inactive members and as you choose words with which to respond to those being visited? (Allow up to 15 minutes for this activity.)

VI. Summary

VII. Assignment
Reread chapter 2 of this book.

VIII. Closing Devotion

## Session 6

I. Introduction
One of Schaller's assumptions quoted on page 55 states: "We assume that if each inactive member has a good reason for being inactive they will continue to be inactive until after that reason has been identified and eliminated."[2] In addition, the entire content of chapter 1 of this book highlights many of the variables which inactives identify as being

instrumental in causing them to be inactive. Therefore it is necessary to consider the strengths and weaknesses of a congregation prior to beginning to visit inactive members and to prepare adequate responses to meet the concerns that inactives identify. The process outlined for this session will assist in preparing visitors to respond helpfully.

II. Objectives

At the conclusion of this learning experience the participants will be able to: (1) articulate their own perceptions of the effectiveness of various aspects of congregational life; (2) list those aspects of the congregation's life that seem least strong and positive; (3) prepare responses which may be effective in addressing the objections of inactive members who cite specific "weak" areas of congregational life that have "caused" them to drop out of congregational life; (4) propose strategies to alert the members of the elected and appointed boards and committees of the congregation to the difficulties, inadequacies, etc., identified by the participants that need to be addressed to reduce negative reactions to aspects of congregational life; (5) propose strategies for using the feedback of the inactive members to assist members of the elected and appointed boards and committees of the congregation to address the negative reactions of inactive members to aspects of congregational life; and (6) outline the plans that the congregation's leaders have already designed and put in place to meet the concerns of inactive members.

III. Supplies needed

Copies of the book, pen/pencil, newsprint/blackboard, magic markers/chalk, masking tape/thumb tacks, and an easel.

IV. Devotion

V. Activities

A. Individually complete the following questionnaire. Note that the statements are made positively. Read each statement carefully. Then respond by choosing one of the five options available to you: (1) Agree Strongly, (2) Agree, (3) Undecided, (4) Disagree, (5) Disagree Strongly. Be as honest and as objective as you are capable of being. (Allow up to 10 minutes for this activity.)

|  | Agree Strongly | Agree | Undecided | Disagree | Disagree Strongly |
|---|---|---|---|---|---|
| 1. Our congregation meets the need for Christian education among | | | | | |
| a. preschool children, | 1 | 2 | 3 | 4 | 5 |
| b. elementary school children, | 1 | 2 | 3 | 4 | 5 |
| c. secondary school youth, | 1 | 2 | 3 | 4 | 5 |
| d. young adults, | 1 | 2 | 3 | 4 | 5 |
| e. middle-aged adults, | 1 | 2 | 3 | 4 | 5 |
| f. older adults. | 1 | 2 | 3 | 4 | 5 |
| 2. Our congregation offers effective group experiences for: | | | | | |
| a. preschool children, | 1 | 2 | 3 | 4 | 5 |
| b. elementary school children, | 1 | 2 | 3 | 4 | 5 |
| c. secondary school youth, | 1 | 2 | 3 | 4 | 5 |
| d. young adults, | 1 | 2 | 3 | 4 | 5 |
| e. middle-aged adults, | 1 | 2 | 3 | 4 | 5 |
| f. older adults. | 1 | 2 | 3 | 4 | 5 |
| 3. Our congregation offers enough different types of group experiences to meet the needs of all our members. | 1 | 2 | 3 | 4 | 5 |
| 4. Our congregation offers ongoing programs which have the following as their principal goal: the support and enrichment of the marriages of our members. | 1 | 2 | 3 | 4 | 5 |
| 5. Our congregation offers ongoing programs which have the following as their principal goal: the support and enrichment of the family life of our members who are living in two-parent family settings. | 1 | 2 | 3 | 4 | 5 |

6. Our congregation offers ongoing programs which have the following as their principal goal: the support and enrichment of the family life of our members who are living in single-parent family settings.　1　2　3　4　5

7. Our congregation offers ongoing programs which have the following as their principal goal: the support and enrichment of the lives of our members who are living in single-person families.　1　2　3　4　5

8. Our congregation offers ongoing programs which have the following as their principal goal: the meeting of the unique needs of our members who are experiencing potential or real marital dissolution.　1　2　3　4　5

9. Our congregation has both the intention and the processes planned and "in place" to manage conflict so that our members grow through re-solved conflicts.　1　2　3　4　5

10. Our congregation is composed of members who are second-, third-, or fourth-generation descendants of families who have been members of our congregation.　1　2　3　4　5

11. The relatives of the members of our congregation are members of our con-gregation or of sister congrega-tions in our denomination.　1　2　3　4　5

| | Agree Strongly | Agree | Undecided | Disagree | Disagree Strongly |
|---|---|---|---|---|---|
| 12. Those members of our congregation who are descendants of families who are not members of our denomination transferred their memberships to our congregation from congregations of our denomination. | 1 | 2 | 3 | 4 | 5 |
| 13. Our congregation employs an effective follow-up procedure to assure that members who move from our community have their church membership transferred quickly to a congregation in their new community. | 1 | 2 | 3 | 4 | 5 |
| 14. The worship life of our congregation is exciting, and it meets the spiritual needs of all the members of our congregation. | 1 | 2 | 3 | 4 | 5 |
| 15. The members of our congregation have positive feelings about the worship life of our congregation. | 1 | 2 | 3 | 4 | 5 |
| 16. The members of our congregation have positive feelings about the preaching they hear from our pulpit. | 1 | 2 | 3 | 4 | 5 |
| 17. The members of our congregation have positive feelings about the quality of the pastoral care they are receiving in crisis situations. | 1 | 2 | 3 | 4 | 5 |

18. The members of our congregation have positive

feelings about the quality of the pastoral care they are receiving through pastoral counseling.  1   2   3   4   5

19. There is agreement between what our pastor perceives to be the needs of the congregation and what the members of our congregation perceive to be the needs of the congregation.  1   2   3   4   5

20. Our congregation has a "soul accounting" system which enables us to monitor the church attendance of our members.  1   2   3   4   5

21. Our congregation has a program which can effectively use the data generated by our "soul accounting" system.  1   2   3   4   5

22. Our congregation's system provides for activating person-to-person contact when a member has not been in church services for four weeks in a row.  1   2   3   4   5

23. Our congregation offers programs which have as their principal goal the assimilating of new members into the life of our congregation.  1   2   3   4   5

24. Our congregation effectively trains, supports, and thanks members who serve in *all* volunteer and leadership positions in the congregation.  1   2   3   4   5

| | Agree Strongly | Agree | Undecided | Disagree | Disagree Strongly |
|---|---|---|---|---|---|
| 25. Our congregation carries on effective and active social ministry programs which are well supported by the members of our congregation. | 1 | 2 | 3 | 4 | 5 |

B. Individually tabulate the number of 1s, 2s, 3s, 4s, and 5s you have circled.
    1. Number of 1s _____
    2. Number of 2s _____
    3. Number of 3s _____
    4. Number of 4s _____
    5. Number of 5s _____
(Allow up to 5 minutes for this activity.)

C. Prior to the session the group facilitator should prepare a grid on sheets of newsprint or blackboard as illustrated below.

|  | A | B | C | D | E | F | G | H | I |
|---|---|---|---|---|---|---|---|---|---|
| 1s | | | | | | | | | |
| 2s | | | | | | | | | |
| 3s | | | | | | | | | |
| 4s | | | | | | | | | |
| 5s | | | | | | | | | |

    1. There should be enough blanks after each number to record individually the tallies of every participant in the group.
    2. The letters A, B, C, etc., represent each of the group participants. (Allow up to 5 minutes for this activity.)
D. Note the number of 4s and 5s which have been circled by each of the participants in the group. As a total group discuss what these numbers seem to mean. (Allow up to 5 minutes for this activity.)
E. Take the next moments and individually write down the number of every statement where you circled a 5. (Note that questions 1 and 2 have a number of subparts. Be specific. For example 1c or 2d.) (Allow 3 minutes for this activity.)
F. Prior to the session the group facilitator should prepare a chart on newsprint or the blackboard that will allow the recording and tallying of each participant's response.

|       | 5s  |       | 4s  |
|-------|-----|-------|-----|
| 1a    |     | 1a    |     |
| 1b    |     | 1b    |     |
| 1c    |     | 1c    |     |

etc. through 25.

G.  As the group facilitator speaks each number in turn, hold up your hand if you have circled a 5 in response to that item.

H.  The group facilitator should count the hands raised in response to each item and record in the first column the number of persons who circled a 5 in response to each item. (Allow up to 5 minutes for this activity.)

I.  Take the next moments and individually write down the number of every statement where you circled a 4. (Allow up to 5 minutes for this activity.)

J.  Tally the numbers of the statements for which the participants circled a 4 and record the count in the second column. (Allow up to 5 minutes for this activity.)

K.  The leaders of the congregation have also done this exercise.

1.  A representative of the leadership of the congregation will now share briefly how their evaluation of the congregation's weaknesses compares to yours.

2.  That representative will briefly outline steps the boards and committees of the congregation have taken and are taking to confront these "weaknesses." (Allow up to 15 minutes for this activity.)

L.  Divide yourselves into small groups of three persons in each group.

1.  Address yourselves to the following questions.

2.  Record your thoughts on a sheet of paper. Clearly indicate which thoughts are addressed to each question.

a.  Question 1, "What kinds of responses can you think of which will help you to talk with inactive members who say that one of the 'weak areas' of the congregation's life 'caused' them to become inactive?"

b.  Question 2, "What strategies can you propose to the members of the elected boards and committees of the congregation to help them correct the 'weak areas' of this congregation's life?" These strategies should be proposed in addition to steps that have been or are being taken as reported earlier to you by a representative of the leadership of the congregation.

c.  Question 3, "What strategies do you propose that could be employed to enable you as visitors to share the feedback you receive while making your calls on inactives?"

3. Give your written comments to the group facilitator at the close of the time allotted to this activity. (Allow up to 25 minutes for this activity.)

M. The group facilitator and the leadership of the congregation will need to work through the comments on these sheets of paper, convey information to the boards and committees of the congregation, and keep the visitors informed about progress that is being achieved.

VI. Summary

VII. Assignment
Come prepared to make visits at our next meeting.

VIII. Closing Devotion


## Sessions 7-16

I. Introduction
Beginning with session 7, visitations will be made on inactive members. The preliminary planning for these visits needs to have been done by the responsible board or committee in concert with the group facilitator prior to the recruitment and training of the visitors.

Decisions that should have been made include answers to questions such as the following:

1. Which inactive members will be visited and in what order will they be visited?

2. Should initial visits on an inactive member be made unannounced or after setting an appointment to meet?

3. How many visitors should be on each visiting team?[3]

Each of the questions above may be answered in a number of ways. Much depends on the local situation. Perhaps it might be wise to do some experimenting initially. However, the group facilitator must know why specific adjustments are being made and must have developed ways to evaluate the effectiveness of the varying approaches.

Furthermore, as visiting teams begin to make calls on inactive members they will need varying kinds of support. Whether that support comes because of the effectiveness of corporate or individual prayer, or because other callers are having similar experiences and are helpful in developing strategies to confront the difficulties and concerns faced by all the visiting teams, or because the congregation's boards and committees are correcting the factors which are motivating members to become inactive, such support is vital both to the success of the program and also to the spiritual and emotional well-being of the visitors.

116

## II. Objectives

At the conclusion of these learning experiences the group participants will be able to: (1) obtain spiritual and emotional support to carry out the ministry of visitation on inactive members; (2) experience growth in their ability to function in this ministry; (3) provide helpful information from inactives to assist leaders of the congregation in enhancing the effectiveness of every aspect of the congregation's ministry; and (4) provide helpful insights to assist fellow visitors to grow in their abilities to serve as visitors of inactive members.

## III. Devotion

## IV. Activities

A. The group facilitator or a member of the group must be prepared to provide some motivation or inspiration for the group prior to the group members making the call(s) they have been assigned on a given evening. (Allow 15 to 20 minutes for this activity.)

B. Each team is given the name(s) of the person(s) they are to visit.

C. Offer a short prayer asking God's blessings on the visitors and on those who will be visited. (Allow 10 minutes for these activities.)

D. Make visits. (Allow not more than 90 minutes for these visits.)

E. Return to the meeting place.

F. The group facilitator should lead the postvisit meeting of the group.

All such debriefing, problem-solving, frustration-venting, etc., postvisit meetings need to be structured carefully. It is very easy for visitors to fall into the trap of gossiping about what they learned while making the calls rather than using the information in a positive way.

If an inactive person says, "The major reason I am not coming to church is because the pastor called on me only once after my wife died. She had given countless hours to serve the congregation, and he could not even honor her memory enough to come and see me more than once," it is important to ask for and receive permission to share that information with the pastor.

What is more, to talk about the state of disarray in the house, the fact of a live-in boyfriend or girlfriend, or a whole host of other subjects is to fall into the trap of gossiping.

Not only is gossiping sinful; it could destroy many of the positive things that visitors are trying to accomplish with inactive people. Since inactive persons normally distrust active members, the reality of gossip, if that reality ever comes to their attention, will cause them to feel justified for distrusting active church members.

G. As concerns arise, the group facilitator may need to: (1) promise to obtain needed information prior to the next meeting, (2) refer group participants to concepts and skills stressed in the first six sessions of the experience, (3) manage difficulties that arise, (4) promise to coordinate items with boards, committees, church office, etc., and (5) facilitate problem solving about any other concern, need, or problem that arises in the group.

V. Summary

VI. Closing Devotion

## Addenda

The training program outlined above does not include preparing visitors to make Gospel presentations. This omission was deliberate. Other books offer comprehensive programs to train individuals to make Gospel presentations.

Although it is important for visitors on inactive members to be able to express their Christian faith, that expression must serve the listening process. The sharing of formal Gospel presentations that are prepared prior to making visits may "get in the way" of effective listening and responding to the concerns of inactive people.

Furthermore if, after spending 8 to 12 hours visiting an inactive person, visitors come to the conclusion that the person has lost his/her faith, it certainly would be a good idea to ask one of the congregation's evangelism calling teams to visit the inactive member to make a Gospel presentation.

The task you are being asked to assume is important. The heavenly Father desires that the lost be reclaimed. Through His Spirit's blessings you can count on His being present to help you fulfill your ministry.

# Notes

### Introduction

1. Lyle Schaller, "Why Church Members Drop Out," *The Lutheran*, XVI (April 5, 1978), 12.
2. Ibid., 14.
3. Andrew M. Greeley, *Crisis in the Church* (Chicago: Thomas More Press, 1979), 255, 256.
4. Dean R. Hoge, "National Contextual Factors Influencing Church Trends," in *Understanding Church Growth and Decline 1950-1978* (New York: The Pilgrim Press, 1979), 120.
5. Greeley, *Crisis in the Church*, 255.

### Chapter 1

1. James Russel Hale, *The Unchurched: Who They Are and Why They Stay Away* (San Francisco: Harper & Row, 1980), 176.
2. Ibid., 167.
3. David A. Roozen and Jackson W. Corrall, "Recent Trends in Church Membership and Participation: An Introduction," in *Understanding Church Growth and Decline 1950-1978* (New York: The Pilgrim Press, 1979), 39—40.
4. Wade Clark Roof, et al., "Factors Producing Growth or Decline in United Presbyterian Congregations," in *Understanding Church Growth and Decline 1950-1978* (New York: The Pilgrim Press, 1979), 222.
5. Ruth T. Doyle and Sheila M. Kelly, "Comparison of Trends in Ten Denominations 1950-75," in *Understanding Church Growth and Decline 1950-1978* (New York: The Pilgrim Press, 1979), 159.
6. David A. Roozen, "Church Dropouts: Changing Patterns of Disengagement and Reentry," *Review of Religious Research*, XXI, 4 (Supplement 1980), 427.
7. Ibid., 442.
8. Ibid.
9. Ibid., 445.
10. Ibid., 443.
11. Ibid.
12. Ibid.
13. Ibid., 434.
14. Ibid., 443.
15. Douglas Walrath, "Response: Why Some People May Go Back to Church," *Review of Religious Research*, XXI, 4 (Supplement 1980), 469—70.

16. Dean R. Hoge, "National Contextual Factors Influencing Church Trends," in *Understanding Church Growth and Decline 1950-1978* (New York: The Pilgrim Press, 1979), 120.
17. Ibid., 120
18. Roozen, "Church Dropouts," 437.
19. Ibid., 446.
20. Dean R. Hoge and David A. Roozen, "Research on Factors Influencing Church Commitment," in *Understanding Church Growth and Decline 1950-1978* (New York: The Pilgrim Press, 1979), 64.
21. Roozen, "Church Dropouts," 446.
22. Warren J. Hartman, *Membership Trends: A Study of Decline and Growth in the United Methodist Church 1949-1975*, cited by Hoge and Roozen, *Understanding Church Growth and Decline* (New York: Pilgrim Press, 1979), 65.
23. Ibid.
24. John S. Savage, *The Apathetic and Bored Church Member: Psychological and Theological Implications* (Pittsford, N.Y.: LEAD Consultants, 1976), 3.
25. Ibid.
26. Ibid., 5.
27. Ibid., 7.
28. Ibid., 70.
29. Hoge and Roozen, "Research on Factors Influencing Church Commitment," 66.
30. Lyle Schaller, "Why Church Members Drop Out," *The Lutheran*, XVI, 6 (April 5, 1978), 12.
31. Lee Lorenz, *The New Yorker*, XLIV, 50 (Feb. 1, 1969), 80.
32. Hale, *The Unchurched*, 174.
33. Walrath, "Response," 472.
34. Andrew M. Greeley, *Crisis in the Church* (Chicago: Thomas More Press, 1979), 255.
35. Ibid., 68—69.
36. Ibid., 69.
37. Ibid., 256.
38. Schaller, "Why Church Members Drop Out," 12.
39. Ibid.
40. Greeley, *Crisis in the Church*, 41—42.
41. Bruce Hunsberger, "A Reexamination of the Antecedents of Apostasy," *Review of Religious Research*, XXI, 2 (Spring 1980), 168.
42. Donald L. Metz, "The Invisible Member: A Report on Inactive Methodists," multilithed (Berkeley: California Bureau of Community Research, 1965), cited by Hoge and Roozen, *Understanding Church Growth and Decline*, 66.
43. R. D. Vangerud, "Meanings in Geographical Mobility and Implications for Pastoral Response," *Pastoral Psychology*, XXIII (September 1972), 17.
44. Roozen, "Church Dropouts," 436.
45. Carl S. Dudley, *Where Have All Our People Gone?: New Choices for Old Churches* (New York: Pilgrim Press, 1979), 77—78.
46. Ibid., p. 77.
47. Hoge and Roozen, "Research on Factors Influencing Church Commitment," 66.
48. Ibid., 65.
49. Lyle Schaller, *Assimilating New Members* (Nashville: Abingdon Press, 1978), 16.
50. Schaller, "Why Church Members Drop Out," 12.
51. Ibid., 13.
52. Ibid., 14.
53. Edward A. Rauff, *Why People Join the Church: An Exploratory Study* (New York: Pilgrim Press, 1979), 207.
54. Dudley, *Where Have All Our People Gone?* 78.
55. Greeley, *Crisis in the Church*, 58.
56. Ibid., 97.

57. Rauff, *Why People Join the Church*, 207.
58. Morton S. Enslin, "Religion Without Theology," *Religion in Life*, XLV, 1 (Spring 1976), 71.
59. Schaller, "Why Church Members Drop Out," 12.
60. Ibid., 13.
61. Greeley, *Crisis in the Church*, 97.
62. Rauff, *Why People Join the Church*, 207.
63. David A. Womack, *The Pyramid Principle of Church Growth* (Minneapolis: Bethany Fellowship, Inc., 1977), 15—16.
64. Hoge and Roozen, "Research on Factors Influencing Church Commitment," 65.
65. Schaller, "Why Church Members Drop Out," 13.
66. Hoge and Roozen, "Research on Factors Influencing Church Commitment," 65.
67. Dudley, *Where Have All Our People Gone?*, 78.
68. Hoge and Roozen, "Research on Factors Influencing Church Commitment," 66.
69. Hale, *The Unchurched*, 174.
70. Ibid., 175—76.
71. Ibid.
72. Hoge and Roozen, "Research on Factors Influencing Church Commitment," 65.
73. Dudley, *Where Have All Our People Gone?* 11—12.
74. Womack, *The Pyramid Principle of Church Growth*, 23.
75. Rauff, *Why People Join the Church*, 64.
76. Peggy Shriver, "Polling the 'Unchurched,' " *Christianity and Crisis*, XXXVIII, 12 (August 21, 1978), 203.
77. Ibid.
78. C. Peter Wagner, *Your Church Can Be Healthy* (Nashville: Abingdon, 1979), 119—20.
79. Dudley, *Where Have All Our People Gone?* 111.
80. Hale, *The Unchurched*, 31.
81. Schaller, "Why Church Members Drop Out," 13.
82. Ibid.
83. Ibid., 12—13.

### Chapter 2

1. Perhaps one of the most cogent arguments for perceiving the body of Christ, the church, to be an organism and not an organization is presented in Lawrence O. Richards and Clyde Hoeldtke's book, *A Theology of Church Leadership* (Zondervan, 1980).
2. Richard G. Hutcheson, *Mainline Churches and the Evangelicals* (Atlanta; John Knox Press, 1981), 115.
3. Ibid.
4. Vernard Eller, *The Outward Bound* (Grand Rapids: Wm. B. Eerdmans Publ. Co., 1980), 62.
5. Lyle Schaller's book, *Assimilating New Members* (Nashville: Abingdon Press, 1978), is very helpful in identifying ways to better assimilate new members.
   Win and Charles Arn address the issue of incorporating new members in chapter seven of their book, *The Master's Plan for Making Disciples* (Pasadena, Calif.: Church Growth Press, 1982). According to these authors, individuals who have been successfully incorporated will exhibit at least nine characteristics. Such a person: (1) identifies with the goals of the church, (2) is regular in worship attendance, (3) feels a sense of spiritual growth and progress, (4) has taken necessary steps of affiliation with the Body, (5) has new friends in the church, (6) has a task or role appropriate to his/her spiritual gifts, (7) is involved in a fellowship group, (8) regularly tithes to the church, and (9) is participating in the Great Commission (pp. 153—58).
6. Lyle Schaller, "Why Church Members Drop Out," *The Lutheran*, XVI (April 5, 1978), 14.
7. Ibid.

8. Using the data orginally gathered for writing *A Study of Generations*, Milo Brekke asked some questions of the data which were not asked when Merton Strommen and his colleagues wrote their important work on American Lutherans. One conclusion of Brekke's study was that children and youth who had experienced education in a Lutheran elementary and/or secondary school tended to be more active in parish life during their adult years than individuals who did not attend a Lutheran School. Milo Brekke, *How Different Are People Who Attended Lutheran Schools?* (St. Louis: Concordia Publishing House, 1974), 119.
9. Schaller, "Why Church Members Drop Out," 14.
10. Douglas Alan Walrath, *Leading Churches Through Change* (Nashville: Abingdon Press, 1979), 62.
11. Hutchenson, *Mainline*, 113.
12. Carl S. Dudley, *Where Have All Our People Gone?* (New York: Pilgrim Press, 1979), 71.
13. Edward A. Rauff, *Why People Join the Church* (New York: Pilgrim Press; Washington D.C.: Glemmary Research, 1979), 201.
14. John R. W. Stott, "Unhooked Christians," *Christianity Today*, XXII, 1 (Oct. 7, 1977), 41.
15. Dudley, *Where Have All Our People Gone?* 67.
16. Stott, "Unhooked Christians," 40.
17. Walrath, *Leading Churches Through Change*, 31.
18. Ibid.
19. Ibid., 101.
20. Ibid.
21. Ruth T. Doyle, "Comparison of Trends in Ten Denominations 1950-75," in *Understanding Church Growth and Decline 1950-1978* (New York: The Pilgrim Press, 1979), 159.
22. Joanne Eisenberg, "Caring for Infants and Toddlers," *District Digest of the Southern California District of the Lutheran Church*, XVI, 7 (August-September 1982), 16.
23. David A. Roozen and Jackson W. Corrall, "Recent Trends in Church Membership and Participation: An Introduction," in *Understanding Church Growth and Decline 1950-1978* (New York: The Pilgrim Press, 1979), 35.
24. Hutchenson, *Mainline*, 112.
25. Rauff, *Why People Join the Church*, 76.
26. Dudley, *Where Have All Our People Gone?* 42.
27. David A. Roozen, "Church Dropouts: Changing Patterns of Disengagement and Re-Entry," *Review of Religious Research*, XXI, 4 (Supplement 1980), 430.
28. Dudley, *Where Have All Our People Gone?* 35—36.
29. Ibid., 38—39.
30. Ibid., 39.
31. H. Richard Niebuhr, *Christ and Culture* (New York: Harper & Brothers, 1951), 83—116.
32. Ibid., 190—230.
33. Hutchenson, *Mainline*, 56.
34. Ibid.
35. John P. O'Hara, "A Research Note on the Sources of Adult Church Commitment Among Those Who Were Regular Attenders During Childhood," *Review of Religious Research*, XXI, 4 (Supplement 1980), 467.
36. Schaller, "Why Church Members Drop Out," 14.
37. Charles J. Keating, *The Leadership Book* (New York: Paulist Press, 1978), 26.
38. Schaller, "Why Church Members Drop Out," 14.
39. Ibid.
40. Ibid.
41. Carl S. Dudley, *Making the Small Church Effective* (Nashville: Abingdon Press, 1978), 112—13.
42. Ibid., 57, 58.
43. G. Douglass Lewis, *Resolving Church Conflicts* (New York: Harper & Row, 1981), 14.

44. "Seminarians Unprepared for Parish 'Give and Take,' " *Reporter*, VI, 5 (Feb. 11, 1980), 4.
45. Lewis, *Resolving Church Conflicts*, 19.
46. Donald L. Metz in his book *New Congregations: Security and Mission in Conflict* (Philadelphia: The Westminster Press, 1967) helpfully describes how various pressures cause newly formed congregations to try to avoid conflict by opting for the security goals of gathering membership, erecting physical structures, and developing financial bases instead of working through the conflicts inherent in the development and attainment of mission goals centering around fellowship, nurture, servanthood, and living the sacrificial life. Metz discovered that once the survival goals were attained and the survival of the congregation seemed no longer in doubt, then the conflicts reemerged concerning how the mission goals were to be lived out by the congregation. Metz suggests that it is possible to forestall this ultimate conflict if the founders of new congregations work through the conflict involved in identifying the mission goals early in the congregation's life rather than deferring this for a later time.
47. Lewis, *Resolving Church Conflicts*, 18.
48. Ibid., 30.
49. Speed Leas has written and lectured on the subject of conflict management within the lives of congregations. In a little work entitled *A Lay Person's Guide to Conflict Management* (Washington: The Alban Institute, 1979), Leas states that conflicts can be resolved by answering the following questions: "What is conflict?" "What do people fight about?" "Why do people fight?" "What do people do that is not helpful when they fight in church?" "What attitudes will help you manage the conflict?" "What are the goals of the conflict management process?" "What can you do to help manage conflict?"
50. Lewis, *Resolving Church Conflicts*, 49.
51. Ibid., 54.
52. Ibid., 58.
53. Ibid., 60.
54. Ibid., 63.
55. Ibid., 66.
56. This feeling will be a great asset for the teamwork that is necessary to complete other group projects. But perhaps the greatest value of all is that the people will work harder to reach the objective of the agreed-upon resolution because people always tend to expend more efforts meeting their own rather than other people's goals.

    Utmost care needs to be exercised when employing a collaborative conflict resolution style. Emphasis must be placed on making certain that members of all conflicting parties feel that their needs or concerns have been addressed adequately and that all are satisfied with how the conflict has been resolved. Sometimes this collaborative style is called "building or achieving consensus." Hutchenson warns against becoming a "consensus congregation." Hutchenson has in mind a specific pejorative definition for the term "consensus." For him consensus means a deliberate policy by those in the majority to get rid of all who disagree with them. This process can include denying leadership positions to members of minority parties, screening new members to make sure their basic attitudes agree with those of the majority party, demanding in subtle ways that dissidents conform or get out of the congregation, and wearing down the opposition until they lose heart and transfer their membership. Hutchinson's alternative for such a "consensus congregation" is a congregation which plans for pluralism. In his words, it is a congregation which chooses to be "both-and rather than either-or." Hutchenson, *Mainline*, 141—42.
57. Lewis, *Resolving Church Conflicts*, 68.
58. Other ways to talk about conflict management styles are 1. win/lose, 2. accommodation, 3. avoidance, 4. compromise, and 5. win/win. Ibid., 77—78.
59. Ibid., 72. Additional helpful material concerning dealing with conflict in congregations

can be garnered from *Church Fights: Managing Conflict in the Local Church*, written by Speed Leas and Paul Kittlaus and published by Westminster Press in 1973, and from an article by W. Th. Janzow entitled "Social and Psychological Forces Present in Conflict in the Church," which appeared in *Issues in Christian Education*, VIII, 3 (Summer, 1974), 5—11.

60. Schaller, "Why Church Members Drop Out," 14.
61. James G. Hougland and James Wood, "Control in Organizations and the Commitment of Members," *Social Forces*, LIX, 1 (September 1980), 93.
62. Schaller, "Why Church Members Drop Out," 14.
63. Everette L. Perry, James H. Davis, Ruth T. Doyle, and John E. Dyble, "Toward a Typology of Unchurched Protestants," *Review of Religious Research*, XXI, 4 (Supplement 1980), 391.
64. Wade C. Roof, Dean R. Hoge, John E. Dyble, and C. Kirk Hadaway, "Factors Producing Growth or Decline in United Presbyterian Congregations," in *Understanding Church Growth and Decline 1950-1978* (New York: The Pilgrim Press, 1979), 221—22.
65. Dudley, *Where Have All Our People Gone?* 112.
66. James C. Hefley *Unique Evangelical Churches* (Waco, Tex.: Word Books, 1977).

## Chapter 3

1. Gerhard Knutson, *Ministry to Inactives* (Minneapolis: Augsburg Publ. House, 1979), 12. Reprinted from *Ministry to Inactives*, by Gerhard Knutson, c 1979, by permission of Augsburg Publishing House.
2. Martin Luther, Smalcald Articles, III, ii, 1-5, in *The Book of Concord*, edited by Theodore Tappert (Philadelphia; Fortress Press, 1959), 303.
3. Lyle E. Schaller, *Assimilating New Members* (Nashville: Abingdon Press, 1959), 117.
4. Ibid. From *Assimilating New Members*, by Lyle E. Schaller. Copyright 1978 by Lyle E. Schaller. Used by permission of the publisher, Abingdon Press.
5. Donald L. Metz, *New Congregations: Security and Mission in Conflict* (Philadelphia: The Westminster Press, 1967), 93.
6. Elizabeth O'Connor, *Call to Commitment* (New York: Harper & Row, 1963), 29—30.
7. Schaller, *Assimilating*, 117.
8. Ibid.
9. Ibid., 118.
10. Ibid.
11. Jack R. Gibb, "Defensive Communication," in *Messages: A Reader in Human Communication*, ed. Jean M. Civikly (New York: Random House, 1974), 332.
12. Ibid.
13. Ibid., 333—37.
14. Ibid.
15. Douglas Walrath, "Response: Why Some People May Go Back to Church," *Review of Religious Research*, XXI, 4 (Supplement 1980), 471.
16. Schaller, *Assimilating*, 118.
17. Lyle E. Schaller, *Hey, That's Our Church* (Nashville: Abingdon Press, 1975), 120—21.
18. Schaller, *Assimilating*, 118.
19. Robert L. Montgomery, "Are You a Good Listener?" *Nation's Business*, LXIX, 10 (October 1981), 65—66, 68.
20. Lyman K. Steil, "Secrets of Being a Better Listener," *U. S. News and World Report*, LXXXVIII, 20 (May 26, 1980), 65—66.
21. "I'm Listening," *Current Health*, V, 9 (May 1979), 26—28.
22. Judith Viorst, "May I Have Your Attention Please?: Eight Thoughts on the Fine Art of Listening," *Redbook*, CLIII, 5 (September 1979), 52, 72.
23. Alic Fryling, "How Do You Care?" *Christianity Today*, XXVI, 12 (July 16, 1982), 16—18.

24. Schaller, *Assimilating*, 118.
25. Ibid.
26. John S. Savage, *The Apathetic and Bored Church Member* (Pittsford, N.Y.: LEAD Consultants, 1976), 97.
27. "The Rite of Friendship" makes use of "Attendance Registration" forms which can be purchased from Universal Book Binders, P. O. Box 159, San Antonio, Tex. 78206. Pads of these tear-off forms are placed in red booklets which are also available from this San Antonio source. Normally provisions are made to place one such booklet and its enclosed pad in every pew. Sometime during each worship service, frequently during the time period prior to the gathering of the offerings, the individual seated nearest to the center aisle in every pew writes his/her name, indicates whether he/she is a member of a church, provides the name and address of his/her present church, and then passes the book to the person sitting next to him/her in the pew. This process continues until every person in each pew has written down the requested information. Individual worshipers are encouraged not only to provide the necessary information but also to read the information provided by all the other persons in the pew. This allows people to get to know the names of other people and makes it possible for them to match names and faces. This latter benefit is what causes the process to be called "The Rite of Friendship." Once all the people have provided the information the completed sheets are torn off the pads and the ushers collect them. It is a simple matter for someone to record the attendance of every person present at each worship service and provide over the weeks and months an accurate profile of attendance patterns of individual members of the congregation.
28. Schaller, *Assimilating*, 119.
29. Ibid., 29—30, 99—115.
30. Ibid., 119.
31. Savage, *The Apathetic and Bored Church Member*, 15—32.
32. Ibid., 93.
33. Schaller, *Assimilating*, 119—20.
34. Savage, *The Apathetic and Bored Church Member*, 97.
35. Ibid.
36. Ibid., 98.
37. Schaller, *Assimilating*, 120.
38. John E. Biersdorf, *Hunger for Experience: Vital Religious Communities in America* (New York: Seabury Press, 1975), 83—84.
39. Schaller, *Assimilating*, 120.
40. Ibid., 120—21.
41. Walrath, "Response," 473, and Wade Clark Roof and Dean R. Hoge, "Church Involvement in America: Social Factors Affecting Membership and Participation," *Review of Religious Research*, XXI, 4 (Supplement 1980), 424.
42. Walrath, "Response," 474.
43. Ibid.
44. Edward A. Rauff, *Why People Join the Church: An Exploratory Study* (New York: Pilgrim Press; Washington, D.C.: Glemmary Research, 1979), 193—94.

### Chapter 4

1. J. Burgess, "The Decline of Discipline," *Dialog*, XII (Summer 1973), 213.
2. Ibid., 213—16.
3. Mark R. Littleton, "Church Discipline: A Remedy for What Ails the Body," *Christianity Today*, XXV, 9 (May 8, 1981), 31.
4. Ronald Sider, "Spare the Rod and Spoil the Church," *Eternity* (October 1976), 53.
5. John Driver, "Forgiveness and Discipline in the Church," *Vital Christianity* (Nov. 13, 1977), 16.
6. E. Heideman, "Church and Christian Discipline," *Reformed Review*, XVI (March 1963), 29.

7. Ibid.
8. Harry G. Coiner, "Living Toward One Another with the Word of God," *Concordia Theological Monthly*, XXXVI (October 1965), 613.
9. Samuel J. Fenn, "One More Look at Matthew 18 (on church discipline)," *Christian Standard*, CXV, 37 (Sept. 14, 1980), 10.
10. Vernard Eller, *The Outward Bound: Caravaning as the Style of the Church* (Grand Rapids: William B. Eerdmans, 1980), 89.
11. Edgar J. Otto, "Church Discipline," in *The Abiding Word*, Vol. II (St. Louis: Concordia Publishing House, 1947), 547.
12. Driver, "Forgiveness and Discipline in the Church," 16, and H. J. A. Bouman, "Biblical Presuppositions for Church Discipline," *Concordia Theological Monthly*, XXX (July 1959), 512.
13. Driver, "Forgiveness and Discipline in the Church," 16.
14. Ibid.
15. Ibid.
16. Martin H. Franzmann, *Follow Me: Discipleship According to St. Matthew* (St. Louis: Concordia Publishing House, 1961), 154.
17. Frank Stagg, "Matthew," in *The Broadman Bible Commentary*, Vol. 8 (Nashville: Broadman Press, 1969), 184.
18. Sider, "Spare the Rod," 19.
19. Ibid.
20. Ibid.
21. Bouman, "Biblical Presuppositions for Church Discipline," 514.
22. Ibid.
23. Ibid.
24. Ibid.
25. Ibid.
26. Coiner, "Living Toward One Another," 639.
27. Edward Earle Ellis, *The Gospel of Luke* (London: Marshall, Morgan and Scott, 1974), 208.
28. Heideman, "Church and Christian Discipline," 31.
29. Driver, "Forgiveness and Discipline in the Church," 16.
30. F. F. Bruce, *1 and 2 Corinthians* (London: Marshall, Morgan and Scott, 1976), 185.
31. Jean Hering, *The Second Epistle of St. Paul to the Corinthians* (London: The Epworth Press, 1967), 15; Alfred Plummer, *A Critical and Exegetical Commentary on the Second Epistle of St. Paul to the Corinthians* (Edinburgh: T and T Clark, 1951), 54; R. V. G. Tasker, *The Second Epistle of Paul to the Corinthians* (Grand Rapids: Wm. B. Eerdmans, 1958), 52.
32. Eller, *The Outward Bound*, 86.
33. A. L. Moore, *1 and 2 Thessalonians* (London: Thomas Nelson and Son LTD, 1969), 120.
34. D. Edmond Hiebert, *First Timothy* (Chicago: Moody Press, 1957), 47.
35. Donald Guthrie, *The Pastoral Epistles: An Introduction and Commentary* (Grand Rapids: Wm. B. Eerdmans, 1957), 69.
36. James Travis, "Discipline in the New Testament," *Pastoral Psychology*, XVI, 159 (December 1965), 19.
37. Augsburg Confession, VII, 2, Tappert, p. 32; Apology VII and VIII, 20, Tappert, p. 171; Apology XIV, 4, Tappert, pp. 214—15.
38. Apology VII and VIII, 3, Tappert, p. 169.
39. Driver, "Forgiveness and Discipline in the Church," 15.
40. Coiner, "Living Toward One Another," 616.
41. Ibid., 619. Harry Coiner's article, entitled "Living Toward One Another with the Word of God," which originally appeared in the October 1965 issue of the *Concordia Theological Monthly*, offers many helpful insights concerning mutual care and discipline in the life of the church.

42. Dietrich Bonhoeffer, *Life Together* (New York: Harper & Row, 1954), 107.
43. Ibid., 105—06.
44. Coiner, "Living Toward One Another," 641.
45. Eller, *The Outward Bound*, 87.
46. Frank Stagg, *New Testament Theology* (Nashville: Broadman Press, 1962), 273.
47. Eller, *The Outward Bound*, 87.
48. Travis, "Discipline in the New Testament," 21.
49. James S. Stewart, *A Man in Christ* (New York: Harper & Brothers, 1935), 196.
50. Charles A. Trentham, "Hebrews," in *The Broadman Bible Commentary*, Vol. 12 (Nashville: The Broadman Press, 1972), 36.
51. Kenneth E. Kirk, *The Vision of God: The Christian Doctrine of the Summum Bonum* (London: Longmans, Green and Co., 1931), 468.
52. Coiner, "Living Toward One Another," 640.

### Chapter 6

1. These five types of statements have been identified and labeled by Drs. Sherrod Miller, Elan Nunnally, and David Wachman and are explained in detail in their book *Alive and Aware: Improving Communication in Relationships*. Minneapolis: Interpersonal Communication Programs, Inc., 1975.
2. Schaller, Lyle E., *Assimilating New Members* (Nashville: Abingdon Press, 1978), 117.
3. James Kennedy, in his *Evangelism Explosion* materials, argues persuasively for three-member visiting teams when making evangelism calls. Three visitors may be overwhelming when making visits on inactive members. Since the initial training event outlined in this book does not assume the availability of visitors who have already been trained, perhaps teams of two visitors each make sense. If trained and experienced visitors are available in subsequent training events, three-member visiting teams may be very worthwhile.

# EIGHTY-EIGHT ASSIGNMENTS FOR DEVELOPMENT IN PLACE

## ENHANCING THE DEVELOPMENTAL CHALLENGE OF EXISTING JOBS

# EIGHTY-EIGHT ASSIGNMENTS FOR DEVELOPMENT IN PLACE

## ENHANCING THE DEVELOPMENTAL CHALLENGE OF EXISTING JOBS

Michael M. Lombardo
Robert W. Eichinger

Center for Creative Leadership
Greensboro, North Carolina

The Center for Creative Leadership is an international, nonprofit educational institution founded in 1970 to foster leadership and effective management for the good of society overall. As a part of this mission, it publishes books and reports that aim to contribute to a general process of inquiry and understanding in which ideas related to leadership are raised, exchanged, and evaluated. The ideas presented in its publications are those of the author or authors.

The Center thanks you for supporting its work through the purchase of this volume. If you have comments, suggestions, or questions about any Center publication, please contact Walter W. Tornow, Vice President, Research and Publication, at the address given below.

Center for Creative Leadership
Post Office Box 26300
Greensboro, North Carolina 27438-6300

CENTER FOR CREATIVE LEADERSHIP

CCL No. 136
ISBN 1-882197-20-8

# Table of Contents

# How to Use This Article

This article is intended as a tool for managers and professionals at all levels and for human resources professionals. Its purpose is to help you add developmental assignments to current jobs. As implied by the title, the focus is on what can be done without moving people into new jobs, on developmental options that can be exercised in existing jobs to more systematically develop people by providing variety in leadership challenge and help in learning from these challenges.

The article will offer 88 developmental experiences that can be added to existing jobs. After reading this, you will have a basis for matching the developmental needs of subordinates to the experiences most likely to address those needs. You will also be able to give subordinate managers the information they need to take charge of their own development more systematically.

As a manager responsible for the development of subordinates, this article will help you take a look at your own job and perhaps find pieces of it that are no longer developmental for you but which might be developmental for one or more of your subordinates. Handing off these parts of your job can lead to development for your subordinates and free you to enhance your own development as well.

The article is organized in five major sections:

| Section | Pages | Contents |
| --- | --- | --- |
| 1 | 1-3 | Background: Discussion of the experiences that our research found to be most developmental to managers and what can be learned from these experiences. |
| 2 | 3-5 | Discussion of the eleven challenges common to developmental experiences. |
| 3 | 5-12 | Discussion of options for development in place, including matrix of 88 such options and the likely developmental aspects of each. |
| 4 | 13-22 | Considerations in setting up a system for development in place. |
| 5 | 23-28 | How to help managers get the most out of development in place. |

## Background: Experiences That Develop Managers and What Makes Them Developmental

The Center for Creative Leadership's continuing studies[†] of executive growth and development have confirmed and extended the adage that experience is the best teacher.

In these studies we found that variety in leadership challenges—certain jobs, exceptional other people (overwhelmingly bosses), coping with our mistakes, enduring hardships, and coursework at pivotal moments—all contribute to the building and seasoning of managers.

Specific experiences teach specific lessons necessary for success. But it is critical, as T. S. Eliot said, not to ". . . have the experience, and miss the meaning." Managers we studied who went on to become effective executives not only had the experiences but learned lessons from them. Learning was not automatic, only made possible by the encountering of certain challenges.

Armed with this knowledge, development can certainly be a more systematic effort than it has been in the past. By exposing young managers to developmental jobs and developmental bosses, and by helping them become effective learners, we can increase our pool of potential leadership talent for the future and provide more meaningful work for managers.

Several problems get in the way, however the most obvious is that American organizations are hardly in a boom era. Since 1980 the *Fortune* 500 has eliminated 2.8 million jobs, 30 million people have been displaced in restructurings, and entire levels of organizations have disappeared overnight (Peters, 1987).

With the rapid increase of dual-career couples and single heads of households, a trend line projected to rise further beyond the year 2000, many managers are refusing geographic moves. A recent study found that 60% of relocation requests were refused. A human resources director told us the tale of asking nine managers to take a plum developmental assignment in France before he got a taker. With organizations slimming down, the problem of creating challenging assignments is complicated by the fact that there are now fewer developmental jobs. In addition, many companies have slowed moving people around due to cost. What is needed is more than a recounting of the types of assignments that are developmental. What is needed is help with development in place so that challenge and growth can be added to virtually *all* managerial and physical jobs.

---

[†] See References.

This is exactly what this article aims to do. Before we discuss development in place, however, we will take a few pages to look at what makes certain kinds of assignments developmental. Then we will turn to the question of how developmental challenge can be provided in existing jobs.

There are five broad categories of experience that executives generally cite as being potentially developmental:

(1) **Challenging jobs**, because they teach about the subtleties of leadership—starting up or fixing troubled operations, expanding large operations, working on time-limited projects from crises to systems installations. These represent what leaders do. Such jobs teach how to cope with pressure, learn quickly, or deal with problem subordinates. In absolute terms, challenging assignments are the best teacher: They are most likely to be remembered as developmental, and can teach both the greatest variety and the largest number of lessons.

(2) **Other people, mostly bosses**, because they serve as models of values. Exceptional people seemed to create a punctuation mark for executives, either by representing what to be or do, or what not to be or do. Whether by serving as a model of integrity or acumen, poor ethics or avarice, certain bosses exemplify how values play out in management settings.

(3) **Hardships**, because they tell us something about our limits. In our research, managers told of making mistakes, getting stuck in dead-end jobs, having to fire people, and enduring the traumas of life. These events often caused managers to look inward and reflect on their humanity, their resilience, and their flaws.

(4) **Coursework**, because it can serve as a powerful comparison point, a chance to build self-confidence by sizing oneself against managers from other firms. Executives spoke of coursework as a kind of forum for trading tips, picking different problem-solving methods, and comparing themselves with others.

(5) **Off-the-job experiences**, usually relating to community services. Such experiences were often primers in persuasion.

The overall benefit of experience seems to be that each kind can teach something uniquely. Learning from the variety of experience can lead, not to the perfection of becoming a manager for all situations, but to becoming a manager with a sense of balance. The confidence that is often built through coping with challenging job assignments may lead to arrogance unless tempered by a sense of one's own foibles and limits. Toughness—doing what has to be done for the business in spite of the human cost—needs to be balanced by sensitivity to others. Managers must lead and empower others to lead as well.

This recognition of opposites and paradox is hardly guaranteed by experience, only made possible. The implicit model for effectiveness that emerged from our research is that diversity in experiences and striving to learn from experience can lead to the personal balance required to be a leader.

The flip side of the argument also holds: Impoverished experience and/or failure to learn from it is related to derailment, to having one's career involuntarily stalled through demotion, plateauing early, or being fired.

So experience matters greatly for effectiveness in management, but what is it about experience that makes it developmental?

## Eleven Challenges Common to Developmental Experience

In our research, not just any type of experience was recalled as having been developmental. Job changes involving the same people, or similar tasks, or indefinite time frames were rarely cited. Here are the 11 most commonly cited challenges, in rough order of how often they were mentioned. Based on this research, we have concluded that for an experience to be developmental, 5 or more of these imbedded challenges are usually present.

### Eleven Developmental Challenges

1. *Success and failure are both possible and will be obvious to others* (some visible score or end point will tell everyone how things went). Most learning occurs of necessity; and when managers believe that the chance of failure is significant, they are more driven to learn. Challenges ranging from running the company picnic, to planning a new site, to handling a negotiation, offer the chance of success or failure.

2.  *Requires aggressive individual, "take charge" leadership.* This
    means there is a need to create visions for change, focus on
    mutual expectations, and learn quickly. Stand-alone assignments
    require managers to be individually accountable, not just
    implementers or part of a team. Examples include hiring a secre-
    tarial pool or dealing with a business crisis.

3.  *Involves working with new people, a lot of people, or both.* Many
    executives in our study reported developing an understanding of
    others from working with unusual groups—foreign governments,
    unions, multi-functional task forces, or problem subordinates.

4.  *Creates additional personal pressure,* such as that caused by
    tough deadlines, high stakes, large scope/scale to job, heavy travel
    or longer hours, highly charged task. Such pressure creates a
    tension between where managers are and where they'd like to be,
    which increases the probability of learning.

5.  *Requires influencing people, activities, and factors over which the
    manager has no direct authority or control,* including such things
    has having superiors besides your boss, or learning to exercise
    lateral influence with peers and outside parties. This challenge
    tests and develops negotiation skills. Many projects, off-the-job
    experiences, and negotiations feature this challenge.

6.  *Involves high variety,* including factors such as working at a
    hectic pace, needing to get large amounts of information orally,
    coping with ambiguity and change, encountering uncontrollable
    events, and managing contradiction and paradox. New situations
    with which the manager is unfamiliar and doesn't know what to
    do, such as crises, building a new team, or strategic assignments,
    can help develop more comfort with ambiguity and the ability to
    juggle multiple problems.

7.  *Will be closely watched by people whose opinions count,* such as
    the boss, higher management, or "outsiders." Important projects,
    crises, and deadline situations are often closely monitored. Such
    situations can develop managers' political skills.

8. *Requires building a team, starting something from scratch, or fixing or turning around a team or an operation or project in trouble.* This includes features such as downsizing, restructuring, layoffs, subordinate issues/problems, a poor-performing unit, and assessing people. Such challenges are commonly demanded in middle- and upper-level leadership jobs and require a broad array of management skills, especially resourcefulness.

9. *Has a major strategic component and is intellectually challenging.* Many staff assignments and major project assignments help enhance the ability to think strategically and grapple with ill-defined, murky areas.

10. *Involves interacting with an especially good, or bad, boss.* Bosses play significant roles in demonstrating what to do (or what not to do) and provide the nearest examples of what values the organization really rewards or punishes. Having variety in bosses helps managers get a stronger sense of how to put their own values into action so they can be more effective managers.

11. *Something important is missing,* including things such as top management support, alignment with strategy, key skills, technical knowledge, or credentials and credibility. The absence of such key elements in an assignment practically compels a manager to learn. When encountered for the first time, many assignments feature a crucial "missing piece."

## Assignments for Development in Place

It is not necessary to change someone's job to provide many of these challenges, although job change is the best method. Adding these challenges to a manager's current job creates new challenges and gives the incumbent a "new job" of sorts.

On the following pages are 88 options for development in place. These are divided into five categories according to the general type of assignment, as described below.

A. **Small projects and start-ups**, which emphasize persuasion, learning new content quickly, working under time pressure, and dealing with groups of people not worked with before. Such assignments may or may not emphasize individual leadership, depending on whether or not the manager is in charge. Tim Hall found in his work with an engineering organization that "plateaued project engineers reported more recognition, more challenge, more psychological success, and more job involvement than their non-plateaued counterparts in technical and administrative areas" (Hall, 1988). This was because the work of the plateaued engineers was broader, more applied, and every project was new and demanded learning. Projects and start-ups which involve a new task, a start-to-finish mandate, and end-result accountability can be powerful experiences. The executives we studied recalled projects as demanding that they learn new content quickly by relying on other people and by appreciating the perspectives of other people. They reported similar benefits from small start-ups, with the added bonus of being held personally accountable.

B. **Small scope jumps and fix-its**, which emphasize team-building, individual responsibility, dealing with the boss, development of subordinates, and time pressure. Seasoned executives rarely talk about team-building in an abstract sense. They specify what kind of situation a team must be built in. Are subordinates green, balky, competent, not competent, former peers? Is the manager an expert or not? Are subordinates experts or not? Are business conditions expanding, troubled, static? Each challenge has a different timbre to it—both in the variety of issues a manager must deal with and in the progression of one's responsibilities. In the project and start-up category, managers may or may not be in charge, but in this second category, they must be in charge for significant challenge to occur. Here they are in charge of people for a short period of time or are responsible for dealing with a specific crisis or problem (an "undoable" project, outplacement, cost-cutting) where high conflict is likely.

   So although similar in nature to the first category, this category emphasizes dealing with emotionally charged situations where motivating and developing others is often required.

C. **Small strategic assignments**, which emphasize intellectual pressure, influence skills, and a lack of credibility in some area. In this category, managers may or may not be closely watched, depending on the assignment. The executives we studied told us that such assignments often shocked them out of a parochial point of view by requiring them to go from an operational to a strategic perspective, from concrete to abstract, or from a present to a future orientation.

Such assignments were also reported as a prime source of learning about coping with ambiguous, uncertain situations in which there is little control and few rules. Having to report on findings and attempting to influence higher level managers should be a feature of such assignments.

D. **Coursework and coaching assignments**, which emphasize missing something one needs to know and intellectual pressure, either of which can lead to heightened self-awareness. Executives in our study recalled how difficult it was to teach or coach others. If they were expert in the area, the difficulty often lay in explaining what had become intuitive for them. If they were not expert (in designing a course, for example), they were likely to feel strong intellectual pressure. From either circumstance, a likely benefit was heightened awareness of what they valued, how they thought, how they re-sponded to intellectual pressure.

When they were on the other side of the situation, similar benefits could accrue. When they attended courses aimed at self-awareness or new content, or when they worked with a higher level manager who was particularly good (or bad) at something, the executives we studied reported reflecting on their values and learning patterns through their exposure to powerful models. These models might be instructors, other participants, a formal model (of problem solving, for example), or a higher level manager who exemplified what to do or what not to do.

Any of these could trigger a look within—an examination of how they did things and what they valued.

E. **Activities away from work**. Development certainly doesn't have to occur on the job. Executives in our study mentioned volunteer work, community service, professional organizations, and coaching children's sports. Any of these tend to emphasize individual leader-ship and working with new people; they may also have elements of learning to influence and persuade.

# EIGHTY-EIGHT ASSIGNMENTS FOR DEVELOPMENT IN PLACE

## Likely Developmental Aspects

| | | Success/Failure | Individual Lead | New People | Pressure | Influence | High Diversity | Closely Watched | Challenge | Strategic | Boss | Missing Something |
|---|---|---|---|---|---|---|---|---|---|---|---|---|
| **A.** | **Small Projects and Start-ups** (see page 6 for general description) | | | | | | | | | | | |
| 1. | Task force on a pressing business problem | X | | X | X | X | | X | | X | | X |
| 2. | Plan a new site | X | X | X | X | | | | | | | |
| 3. | Plan an off-site meeting, conference, convention | X | | X | X | | | | | | | |
| 4. | Handle a negotiation with a customer | X | X | | X | X | | | | | | X |
| 5. | Install a new system | X | X | X | X | X | | X | | | | X |
| 6. | Work with a plant shut down crew | X | X | X | X | | | X | X | | | X |
| 7. | Integrate systems across units | X | X | X | X | | | X | | | | X |
| 8. | Supervise product, program, equipment, or systems purchase | X | X | | X | X | X | | | | X | X |
| 9. | Supervise liquidation of product, program, equipment, or system | X | X | | X | X | X | | | | X | X |
| 10. | Present proposal report to top management | X | | X | X | X | | X | | X | X | |
| 11. | Go off-site to troubleshoot problems (deal with dissatisfied customer) | X | X | X | X | X | X | | X | | | X |
| 12. | Go to campus as recruiter | | | X | | X | X | | | | | X |
| 13. | Supervise a study team | | X | X | | X | | | | | | |
| 14. | Run company picnic | X | X | | X | X | X | | | | | |
| 15. | Start up something small (e.g., hire a secretarial pool) | X | X | X | X | | X | | X | | X | X |
| 16. | Run a task force on a business problem | X | X | X | X | X | X | X | | | | X |
| 17. | Business trip to foreign country | | | X | | X | X | | | | | X |
| 18. | Lobby for the organization | | | X | X | X | X | | | | | X |
| 19. | Supervise furnishing of offices | X | | X | | X | X | X | | | | |

# EIGHTY-EIGHT ASSIGNMENTS FOR DEVELOPMENT IN PLACE (cont.)

## Likely Developmental Aspects

| | Success/Failure | Individual Lead | New People | Pressure | Influence | High Diversity | Closely Watched | Challenge | Strategic | Boss | Missing Something |
|---|---|---|---|---|---|---|---|---|---|---|---|
| **A. Small Projects and Start-ups** (cont.) | | | | | | | | | | | |
| 20. Supervise assigning office space | X | | X | | X | X | X | | | | |
| 21. Make speeches for organization | X | | X | X | X | | | | | | X |
| 22. Write PR releases | X | | X | | X | | | | | | |
| 23. Serve at booth at trade show | | | X | | X | | | | | | |
| 24. Work with credit union board or committee | | | X | | X | | | | | | |
| 25. Be a loaned executive | | X | X | X | X | X | | | | | |
| 26. Serve on new project/product review committee | | | X | | X | X | X | | X | | X |
| 27. Work short periods in other units | | | X | X | X | X | | | | | X |
| 28. Do a project with another function | | | X | X | X | X | | | | | X |
| 29. Manage renovation project | X | X | X | X | X | X | | | | | |
| 30. Launch new product/program | X | X | X | X | X | X | X | | | | X |
| 31. Use seed budget on personal idea/project | X | X | | | X | X | | | | X | X |
| 32. Follow a new product/system through entire cycle | | | X | X | X | X | | X | X | | X |
| 33. Represent concerns of non-exempt employees to higher management | X | X | X | X | X | X | | | | | |
| 34. Assign project with tight deadline | X | X | X | X | | X | X | | | X | |
| 35. Manage the visit of a VIP | X | | X | X | | X | X | | | X | |
| 36. Serve on a junior board | | | X | X | X | X | | | X | | X |
| **B. Small Scope Jumps and Fix-its** (see page 6 for general description) | | | | | | | | | | | |
| 37. Create symbol/rallying cry for change and implementation | X | X | | | X | | | | | | |

## EIGHTY-EIGHT ASSIGNMENTS FOR DEVELOPMENT IN PLACE (cont.)

**Likely Developmental Aspects**

| B. Small Scope Jumps and Fix-its (cont.) | Success/Failure | Individual Lead | New People | Pressure | Influence | High Diversity | Closely Watched | Challenge | Strategic | Boss | Missing Something |
|---|---|---|---|---|---|---|---|---|---|---|---|
| 38. Manage ad hoc group of inexperienced people | x | x | | x | | x | x | x | | x | x |
| 39. Manage ad hoc group of balky people | x | x | | x | | x | x | x | | x | x |
| 40. Manage ad hoc group of low competence people | x | x | | x | | x | x | x | | x | x |
| 41. Manage ad hoc group of former peers | x | x | | x | | x | x | x | | x | x |
| 42. Manage ad hoc group—person is expert, people are not | x | x | | x | | x | x | x | | x | |
| 43. Manage ad hoc group—people are expert, person is not | x | x | | x | | x | x | x | | x | x |
| 44. Manage ad hoc group during a fix-it | x | x | | x | | x | x | x | | x | x |
| 45. Manage ad hoc group in a static operation | x | x | | x | | x | x | x | | x | x |
| 46. Manage ad hoc group in a rapidly expanding operation | x | x | | x | | x | x | x | | x | x |
| 47. Size up who to keep and who to let go | x | x | | | | | | | | | x |
| 48. Deal with a business crisis | x | x | x | x | x | x | x | x | | x | x |
| 49. Assign "undoable" project (last person who tried it failed) | x | x | | x | x | x | x | x | | x | x |
| 50. Supervise outplacement | x | x | | x | | x | x | x | | x | |
| 51. Supervise cost-cutting | x | x | | x | x | x | x | x | | x | |
| 52. Design new, simpler effectiveness measures | x | x | | | x | | x | x | | | x |
| 53. Assign to work on something they hate to do | x | x | | x | | x | x | x | | x | x |
| 54. Resolve conflict among warring subordinates | x | x | | x | | x | | x | | | x |
| 55. Make peace with an enemy | x | x | | x | x | x | | x | | | x |

# EIGHTY-EIGHT ASSIGNMENTS FOR DEVELOPMENT IN PLACE (cont.)

## Likely Developmental Aspects

| | Success/Failure | Individual Lead | New People | Pressure | Influence | High Diversity | Closely Watched | Challenge | Strategic | Boss | Missing Something |
|---|---|---|---|---|---|---|---|---|---|---|---|
| **C. Small Strategic Assignments** (see page for 6 general description) | | | | | | | | | | | |
| 56. Summarize new trend/technique; present to others | x | | | x | x | | | | x | | x |
| 57. Write a proposal for a new system, product, etc. | x | | | x | x | | | | x | | x |
| 58. Spend a week with customers/ write report | x | | x | x | x | | | | x | | x |
| 59. Do a competitive analysis | x | | | x | x | | | | x | | x |
| 60. Write a speech for someone higher in organization | x | | | x | x | | | | x | | x |
| 61. Write up policy statement | x | | | x | x | | | | x | | x |
| 62. Study customer needs | x | | x | x | x | | | | x | | x |
| 63. Postmortem on failed project | x | | x | x | x | | | | x | | x |
| 64. Do a problem prevention analysis | x | | | | x | | | | x | | x |
| 65. Study innovation of customers/ competitors | x | | x | x | x | | | | x | | x |
| 66. Interview outsiders on their view of the organization | x | | x | x | x | | | | x | | x |
| 67. Evaluate impact of training | x | | | x | x | | | | x | | x |
| 68. Construct a success/derailment profile | x | | x | x | x | | | | x | | x |
| 69. Write up contingency scenario | x | | x | x | x | | | | x | | x |
| 70. Work on affirmative action planning | x | | x | x | x | | | | x | | x |
| **D. Coursework/Coaching Assignments** (see page 7 for general description) | | | | | | | | | | | |
| 71. Teach a course or workshop | x | x | x | x | x | | | | | | x |

## EIGHTY-EIGHT ASSIGNMENTS FOR
## DEVELOPMENT IN PLACE (cont.)

### Likely Developmental Aspects

| | Success/Failure | Individual Lead | New People | Pressure | Influence | High Diversity | Closely Watched | Challenge | Strategic | Boss | Missing Something |
|---|---|---|---|---|---|---|---|---|---|---|---|
| **D. Coursework/Coaching Assignments** (cont.) | | | | | | | | | | | |
| 72. Teach someone how to do something they are not expert in | | | | x | | | | | | | x |
| 73. Teach someone how to do something they're expert in | | | | x | | | | | | | x |
| 74. Design training course | x | x | x | x | | | | | | | x |
| 75. Do a self-study project | | | | x | | | | | | | |
| 76. Attend self-awareness course | | | x | x | | | | | | | |
| 77. Train as an assessor in assessment center | | | x | x | | | | | | | x |
| 78. Spend a day with an expert on some job aspect | | | x | x | x | | | | | | x |
| 79. Study new technical area | | | x | x | | | | | | | x |
| 80. Study history/draw business parallels | | | | x | | | | | | | |
| 81. Assign to work with higher manager who is particularly good or bad at something | x | | | x | | | | | | x | x |
| **E. Off-Job Activities** (see page 7 for general description) | | | | | | | | | | | |
| 82. Become active in a professional organization | | x | x | | x | | | | | | |
| 83. Serve with a community agency | | x | x | | x | | | | | | |
| 84. Become active in a volunteer organization | | x | x | | x | | | | | | |
| 85. Join a community board | | x | x | | x | | | | | | |
| 86. Act as a consultant on a problem/issue outside job | | x | x | | x | | | | | | |
| 87. Coach children's sports | x | x | x | | x | | | x | | | |
| 88. Work with a charitable organization | | x | x | | x | | | | | | |

## Setting Up a System for Development in Place

Once developmental assignments have been worked out, there needs to be some method for making specific assignments to specific managers. There also needs to be some way of helping managers learn the most from their developmental assignments and a way to get feedback to them on how effectively they are learning.

### Which Assignments for Which People?

Numerous strategies are available. First, armed with this information, many managers will voluntarily add developmental challenges to their present jobs. They will assess themselves in accordance with what they've done and not done, where they are proficient and where not so proficient.

Second, a general strategy can be followed of exposing early career managers over a period of time to one or two assignments in each of the five areas. More than one in each appropriate category may be advisable because a small project and a small start-up are somewhat different experiences, although for simplicity they are grouped in the same category. Such a strategy allows for a natural building of variety in experience and a progression in responsibilities.

Third, a job assignment which naturally arises through the course of work can be used as a developmental experience. For example, a financial task force requires participation of a staff member. Using the 11 developmental challenges on pages 3-5, the task force can be coded as to its developmental potential, or by referring to pages 6-7 the manager can decide which type of development in place assignment it is (i.e., a project).

Since such projects usually demand learning quickly by relying on other people, persuasion, working under time pressure and dealing with groups not dealt with before, the manager can then ask which of his or her subordinates could benefit most from this assignment. Who has never worked on a short-term project? Who most needs to learn to be a quick study, improve persuasiveness, or learn to deal with pressure better?

Fourth, a strategy of targeted development can be followed where a specific need is addressed by one assignment or a series of assignments. Following are two charts to help target development. The left column of each chart lists the developmental needs (first chart) or the derailment factors (second chart) identified in CCL's studies of learning from experience. The middle column lists assignments for development in place to address the needs. The right column lists some of the 88 assignments by number.

These charts have several general uses: one is to locate multiple assignments in order to build long-term competency for a group of people low in strategic skills, for example; another is to custom-design developmental assignments when none of the 88 development-in-place assignments are currently available or are not appropriate. In this use, managers should refer to the charts to detail what needs to be developed (e.g., strategic skills) and look at the description of strategic assignments on page 6 and the examples on page 11. In this example, what is needed is an assignment which emphasizes intellectual pressure, influence skills with higher management, and missing a needed skill or knowledge. The manager should then ask what important business area or nagging problem could stand a fresh look. For example, he or she might assign one or more people to look into quality problems in their unit, see what other companies are doing, consult with experts, and present recommendations to higher management.

Finally, perhaps the most common use of the following charts is to match assignments with an individual's developmental need or to build a strength in a new area. For example, a person who doesn't sell up well or who has never had to sell an idea to higher management might be assigned to represent concerns of non-exempt employees to higher management (33), serve on a junior board (36), or write up a policy statement for approval (60).

## I. Matching Needs to Development in Place Assignments:
## Skills and Perspectives

| Need | Recommendation | Some Suggested Assignments |
|---|---|---|
| **1. Resourcefulness** | | |
| • Has trouble coping with ambiguity, unstructured problems | Start-ups/projects<br>Fix-its/scopes<br>Strategy | 1, 2, 5, 7, 15, 16, 30<br>42, 43, 48, 49<br>56-59, 67, 69 |
| • Doesn't sell up well | Projects requiring presentation<br>Coaching | 10, 33, 36, 60 |
| • Has trouble setting up systems | Small projects<br>Systems installation | 3, 14, 19, 29<br>5, 7, 8, 11 |
| • Parochial (non-strategic) | Multi-unit projects<br>Switch to line or staff project | 1, 7, 8, 9, 16, 32<br>56-70 |
| **2. Doing Whatever It Takes** | | |
| • Lacks perseverance | Assign to do something they hate to do<br>Assignment with tight deadline<br>Confront conflicts | 47-50, 53-55<br><br>1-11, 19-20, 29, 34, 48<br><br>4, 11, 19, 20, 33, 39, 44 |
| • Doesn't understand likes/dislikes/not particularly open to "new" learning | Coursework/coaching<br>Give a task which is too large to handle alone or where their expertise is limited | 75-77, 81<br>16, 30, 37-46, 48 |
| • Lacks self-confidence/ doesn't take charge willingly | Coursework/coaching<br>Start-ups/team-building situations<br>Off-job | 75,77, 81<br>1, 2, 5, 7, 15, 16, 30, 38-46<br><br>85-87 |
| **3. Quick Study** | | |
| • Studies new topics to death | Presentations requiring "new" information<br>Project with tight deadline<br>Coaching | 10, 33, 36, 39<br><br>1-10<br>81 |

## I. Matching Needs to Development in Place Assignments: Skills and Perspectives (cont.)

| Need | Recommendation | Some Suggested Assignments |
|------|----------------|----------------------------|
| **3. Quick Study (cont.)** | | |
| • Flounders due to lack of technical/functional expertise | Multi-unit project with experts | 1, 27, 28, 43 |
| | Switch to line or staff project with experts | 56-70 |
| | Study combined with work project | 78-80 |
| | Have the person study how he or she can learn new areas quickly | 71-74 |
| | Attend professional meetings on unfamiliar topics | 82 |
| **4. Decisiveness** | | |
| • Lacks decisiveness | Assignment with deadline | 4, 8, 9, 11, 14, 34 |
| • Too quick | Assignment featuring persuasion | 10, 12, 17, 18, 21-25, 33, 35, 36, 43, 57, 60 |
| | Off-job | 82-88 |
| **5. Leading Subordinates** | | |
| • Poor at delegating, motivating | Various team-building situations | 16, 28, 37-46, 87 |
| | Coaching | 81 |
| • Poor at developing | Give a task that is too large to do alone | 16, 30, 37-46, 48 |
| **6. Setting a Developmental Climate** | | |
| • Too controlling/over manages | Various team-building situations | 16, 28, 37-46, 87 |
| | Coaching | 81 |
| • Doesn't lead by example | Give a task that is too large to do alone | 16, 30, 37-46, 48 |

## I. Matching Needs to Development in Place Assignments:
## Skills and Perspectives (cont.)

| Need | Recommendation | Some Suggested Assignments |
|---|---|---|
| **7. Confronting Problem Subordinates** | | |
| • Procrastinates/smoothes over problems | Downsizing/cutback/shutdown | 6, 9, 47-51, 63-64 |
| • Acts too abruptly | Inheriting a problem subordinate or group | 38-44, 47, 54, 55 |
| **8. Team Orientation** | | |
| • Tries to do it all alone | Give a task too large to handle alone | 16, 30, 37-46, 48 |
| | Various team-building situations | 16, 28, 37-46, 87 |
| • Doesn't promote team spirit | Off-job | 83-84, 86-87 |
| **9. Hiring Talented Staff** | | |
| • Doesn't attract good people | Staff a task force or start-up | 16, 30, 37-46 |
| • Hires in own image | Learn what to look for in people | 12, 47, 50, 68, 71, 74 |
| **10. Building and Mending Relationships** | | |
| • Poor negotiator | Assignment with deadline | 4, 8, 9, 11, 14, 34 |
| • Lacks understanding of others | Project (e.g., represent customer concerns to top management) | 10-12, 17, 18, 23-25, 33, 36, 54, 55, 58, 62, 65 |
| | Coursework combined with work assignment | 71, 72, 74-77 |
| | Deal with new group | 38-46, 83-88 |
| • Problems with peers | Assignment requiring peer persuasion | 1, 5, 7, 16, 19, 20, 26-30 |
| | Off-job | 82-88 |

## I. Matching Needs to Development in Place Assignments:
## Skills and Perspectives (cont.)

| Need | Recommendation | Some Suggested Assignments |
|---|---|---|
| **11. Compassion and Sensitivity** | | |
| • Overly critical of mistakes | Project where they lack expertise | 43, 49, 53 |
| • Impersonal | Coaching/coursework | 72, 75-77, 81 |
| | Off-job | 83, 84, 87, 88 |
| • Doesn't listen well | Assign "undoable" project | 47-50, 53-55 |
| | Confront conflicts | 4, 11, 19, 20, 33 |
| | Assign to develop new group | 38-46 |
| **12. Straightforwardness and Composure** | | |
| • Tells people what they want to hear | Coaching/coursework | 72, 75-77, 81 |
| • Becomes cynical/blames others | Make individual accountable in difficult situations | 2, 5, 15, 16, 29-31, 38-40, 44, 48-49, 53-55 |
| **13. Balance Between Personal Life and Work** | | |
| • Overdoes work | Off-job | 83-85, 87-88 |
| | Coursework | 75-76 |
| • Has conflicts between the two | Counsel employees with personal or work problems | 33, 40, 42, 54, 71 |
| **14. Self-awareness** | | |
| • Doesn't seek feedback/ admit mistakes easily | Coursework/coaching | 75-77, 81 |
| • Doesn't know strengths/ weaknesses | Assign "undoable" project or against a specific skills deficiency | 49, 53, 55 |
| **15. Putting People at Ease** | | |
| • Distant/in a hurry | Work with new groups | 1, 4, 5, 7, 38-46, 83-88 |
| • Lack of humor | Coursework | 75-77 |

## I. Matching Needs to Development in Place Assignments:
## Skills and Perspectives (cont.)

| Need | Recommendation | Some Suggested Assignments |
|---|---|---|
| **16. Acting with Flexibility** | | |
| • Driven to be one way or the other (e.g., overly tough, too individually-oriented, too self-confident) | Coaching/coursework<br>Make individual accountable in difficult situations | 75-77, 81<br>2, 5, 15, 16, 29-31, 38-46, 48-49 |

## II. Matching Needs to Development in Place Assignments: Derailment Factors

| Need | Recommendation | Some Suggested Assignments |
|---|---|---|
| **1.  Problems with Interpersonal Relationships** | | |
| • Insensitivity | Project where they lack expertise | 43, 49, 53 |
| | Coaching/coursework | 72, 75-77, 81 |
| | Off-job | 83, 84, 87, 88 |
| | Assign "undoable" project | 47-50, 53-55 |
| | Confront conflicts | 4, 11, 19, 20, 33 |
| | Assign to develop new group | 38-46 |
| • Overambition | Make individual accountable in difficult situations | 2, 5, 15, 16, 29-31, 38-40, 44, 48-49, 53-55 |
| **2.  Problems with Molding a Staff** | | |
| • Poor at developing | Various team-building situations | 16, 28, 37-46, 87 |
| | Coaching | 81 |
| • Overmanages | Give a task that is too large to do alone | 16, 30, 37-46, 48 |
| • Procrastinates | Downsizing/cutback/shutdown | 6, 9, 47-51, 63-64 |
| • Acts too abruptly | Inheriting a problem subordinate or group | 38-44, 47, 54, 55 |
| • Doesn't promote team spirit | Off-job | 83-84, 86-87 |
| • Doesn't attract good people | Staff a task force or start-up | 16, 30, 37-46 |
| • Hires in own image | Learn what to look for in people | 12, 47, 50, 68, 71, 74 |
| **3.  Difficulty in Making Strategic Transitions** | | |
| • Has trouble coping with ambiguity, unstructured problems | Start-ups/projects | 1, 2, 5, 7, 15, 16, 30 |
| | Fix-its/scopes | 42, 43, 48, 49 |
| | Strategy | 56-59, 67, 69 |

## II. Matching Needs to Development in Place Assignments:
## Derailment Factors (cont.)

| Need | Recommendation | Some Suggested Assignments |
|---|---|---|
| **3. Difficulty in Making Strategic Transitions (cont.)** | | |
| • Has trouble setting up systems | Small projects | 3, 14, 19, 29 |
| | Systems installation | 5, 7, 8, 11 |
| • Parochial (non-strategic) | Multi-unit projects | 1, 7, 8, 9, 16, 32 |
| | Switch to line or staff project | 56-70 |
| • Studies new topics to death | Presentations requiring "new" information | 10, 33, 36, 39 |
| | Project with tight deadline | 1-10 |
| | Coaching | 81 |
| • Flounders due to lack of technical/functional expertise | Multi-unit project with experts | 1, 27, 28, 43 |
| | Switch to line or staff project with experts | 56-70 |
| | Study combined with work project | 78-80 |
| | Have the person study how he or she can learn new areas quickly | 71-74 |
| | Attend professional meetings on unfamiliar topics | 82 |
| • Driven to be one way (e.g., overly tough, too individually-oriented, too self-confident) | Coaching/coursework | 75-77, 81 |
| | Make individual accountable in difficult situations | 2, 5, 15, 16, 29-31, 38-46, 48-49 |
| **4. Lack of Follow-through/Untrustworthy** | | |
| • Lacks perseverance | Assign to do something they hate to do | 47-50, 53-55 |
| | Assignment with tight deadline | 1-11, 19-20, 29, 34, 48 |
| | Confront conflicts | 4, 11, 19, 20, 33, 39, 44 |
| • Doesn't understand likes/dislikes/not particularly open to "new" learning | Coursework/coaching | 75-77, 81 |
| | Give a task which is too large to handle alone or where their expertise is limited | 16, 30, 37-46, 48 |
| • Lacks self-confidence/ doesn't take charge willingly | Coursework/coaching | 85-87 |
| | Start-ups/team-building situations | |
| | Off-job | |

## II. Matching Needs to Development in Place Assignments:
## Derailment Factors (cont.)

| Need | Recommendation | Some Suggested Assignments |
|------|----------------|----------------------------|
| **5. Overdependence** | | |
| • Lack of independence | Assignment with deadline | 4, 8, 9, 11, 14, 34 |
| • Lacks breadth | Project (e.g., represent customer concerns to top management) | 10-12, 17, 18, 23-25, 33, 36, 54, 55, 58, 62, 65 |
| | Coursework combined with work assignment | 71, 72, 74-77 |
| | Deal with new group/ technology/function | 38-46, 83-88 |
| • Problems with peers | Assignment requiring peer persuasion | 1, 5, 7, 16, 19, 20, 26-30 |
| | Off-job | 82-88 |
| • Overdependent on boss | Project with different boss | 81 |
| **6. Unable to Adapt to Bosses/Strategy/Culture** | | |
| • Doesn't sell up well | Projects requiring presentation | 10, 33, 36, 60 |
| | Coaching | 81 |
| • Doesn't put people at ease | Coursework/off-job | 75-77, 82-88 |
| • Lack of understanding of complexity of strategy/ cultural issues | Strategy assignments | 56-70 |

## Helping Managers Get the Most From Their Experiences

Learning won't occur by itself when managers are given developmental assignments. It's quite likely that many managers will rely on past habits and try to apply old skills to new situations. This is in fact what often happened, as a group, for the executives we studied who derailed. They relied on comfortable habits, and their learning formed no pattern they could use later. As a result, their management behavior changed little.

For managers to learn something of long-term value to them, they need to specify what sort of transition they are making—from what to what? The essence of this issue is that the manager will have to give up, or at least modify, some comfortable habits in order to grow.

Some transitions feature something the manager has never done before, such as going from a task where things are running smoothly to a disaster or fix-it problem. Other transitions feature a progression—significantly more responsibility in a challenge they have faced before. As an example, some executives who went on to be successful start-up managers at age 40 had mini start-ups earlier in their careers: In their early 20s they hired a secretarial pool; later, they started a small department; in their early 30s they started up a new product; later, they were a second-tier manager in a start-up. By age 40 they were prepared to start up a major department or function.

Typical transitions that developmental assignments may require are:

- From dealing with a problem person to dealing with a problem group

- From team-building with non-experts to team-building with experts (or vice versa)

- From responsibility for a piece of a system or project to responsibility for the whole

- From managing an existing facility to planning the rent or usage of a new one

Specifying the nature of the transition one is making is necessary for targeted development to occur. For example, a first-time project manager might need to make the following transitions and have a strategy for each:

| FROM | TO | SAMPLE STRATEGIES |
|---|---|---|
| 1. Technical expert | Manager of experts from other areas | Seek tutoring; seek counseling on major conceptual umbrellas to organize learning; targeted reading |
| 2. Managing known people | Managing a new group | Set up pilot task to help manager see the group in action (assess their needs and skills, size them up) |
| 3. A well-functioning group | A group where conflict is rife | Have meetings to seek mutual agreements, negotiate ways of working together, isolate conflicts and deal with them |

The danger is always that a new task may be met with old behavior, using management techniques that worked well in the previous situation. Managers need awareness of the developmental transition they are making and a plan for dealing with it.

To gain from the situation, they need not only to try different tasks but also to learn something from their efforts. Some examples of methods of helping managers learn from their experiences are:

_____ seeking tutoring in new technical areas or tutoring in how to handle different leadership challenges

_____ placing them with a role model who exemplifies how to do something well

_____ keeping a learning diary

_____ asking them what they have learned often, and what habits they have that are getting too comfortable for them

_____ having regular dinner meetings with those who face or have faced similar leadership challenges

_____ attending coursework targeted toward self-awareness of strengths, weaknesses, and limits, or which addresses a compelling problem they face on the job at present

_____ having them construct a learning plan (how will they size up people? team build? create a symbol for change or rallying cry? deal with the boss?)

In a brief paper such as this, only cursory treatment can be given to what can be learned from experience. For fuller descriptions of learning, the reader is referred to several publications for assistance in providing managers feedback.[†]

On the issue of effective learning, here are some typical learning differences between managers who derail prematurely because they fail to learn as much as they could from their experiences (or have limited experiences), and those who are excellent learners. Such learners much more often get to executive ranks and stay there, but our purpose here is not to encourage progression, but learning. Several studies have shown that it is not level or income that is related to life satisfaction but, among other reasons, being an active learner who seeks new challenges and learns from them. Our purpose here is development, which helps add excitement and achievement to our lives and gives us a sense of control over our destiny.

The final step in the process of using assignments in place for development is to provide guidance and feedback to managers on how effective they are as learners—what they do to block their learning and what they do to help themselves learn.

--------

[†] *The Lessons of Experience* (McCall, Lombardo, & Morrison), Lexington Books, 1988, covers the original studies of male executives. *Breaking the Glass Ceiling* (Morrison, White, & Van Velsor), Addison-Wesley, 1987, covers the study of female executives. *Key Events in Executives' Lives* (Lindsey, Homes, & McCall), Center for Creative Leadership, 1988, is a detailed technical description of the events and learnings of male executives. *Benchmarks*® (Lombardo & McCauley) is a feedback instrument that assesses the lessons of experience, derailment factors, and the ability to handle challenging jobs.

| **BLOCKS TO LEARNING** | **AIDS TO LEARNING** |
|---|---|
| 1. Focus on results and technical matters. Little attention paid to leadership role. | 1. Focus on results, but leadership challenges are actively sought; such managers often have a learning plan. |
| 2. Over-control may wipe out ambiguity or conflict with quick decisions or go to the other extreme and study problems into the ground. Uncomfortable with the fragmented pace of management work or with "first-time problems." | 2. Develop a tolerance for ambiguity and uncontrollable situations: remain open to different views of the problem, not jump to conclusions, rely on small experiments and feedback from them, taking the time to work through conflicts. |
| 3. Excessive reliance on bosses, high-status figures, or self for counsel. Not particularly open to feedback from others or fail to act on feedback. | 3. Seek feedback from success or failure on tasks. May not seek but are open to feedback from many sources—boss, self, subordinates, peers, customers, etc. Because we show different faces to different people and different work relationships create different leadership dynamics, this 360-degree feedback is invaluable. |
| 4. Habit-bound—have a good sense of what worked in the past and try to repeat it. Like to work with same people, similar functions and technical areas. Show little interest in team-building in new situations or getting a mix of talents in the group. | 4. Focus on the transition from one challenge to another. What habits have gotten too comfortable? What is different about this challenge that requires acting differently? What can be learned from this? |
| 5. Over-generalize—"the way to develop people is . . ." Form precepts and fit new events within them. | 5. Specify what one is learning—for example, nine different people management situations are listed in the 88 assignments because each can be expected to teach a different aspect of team-building. CCL research found that while successful executives had a few general learnings about team-building, they were more likely than the derailed to mention rules of thumb specific to each team-building situation. |

| **BLOCKS TO LEARNING** | **AIDS TO LEARNING** |
|---|---|
| 6. Low self-awareness—not attuned to the interplay of strengths, weaknesses, and limits within self. May be reluctant to express or not know what strong likes and dislikes are. | 6. Develop awareness of what strengths and weaknesses they have and how they are linked together. Some of those who derailed found that a strength such as leading subordinates later became a weakness such as over-managing or a strength such as being creative (with many projects going on at once) might have a corollary weakness which eventually caused problems, including follow-through, lack of attention to essential detail, or leaving people dangling. The recognition of the strengths, weaknesses, and limits that we all have leads to the self-awareness necessary to make transitions to a different way of behaving. Knowing what we like and dislike, what we're good at and how that can hurt as well as help is a key mechanism in helping us change our behavior. |
| 7. Unaware of impact—may get abdicative, passive, dictatorial or abrasive under pressure, yet not know it. | 7. Become aware of interpersonal impact. Through feedback and coursework, come to understand how small day-to-day actions have a large impact on others. |
| 8. Take problems personally—may be seen as emotionally volatile under pressure. | 8. Learn to talk about emotions, likes and dislikes, without over-reacting. Stability under pressure and composure differentiated successful from derailed executives in the CCL studies. |
| 9. Promotion-oriented—may openly plan for next job, politic, not be particularly demanding of subordinates, which may leave them undeveloped. | 9. Focus on solving problems in the job they're in rather than ticket punching for the future. Successful executives we studied were more likely to focus on present challenges, be quite demanding of subordinates, and, partly because of that, often developed the talent beneath them. |

| **BLOCKS TO LEARNING** | **AIDS TO LEARNING** |
|---|---|
| 10. Doesn't handle mistakes well—may sandbag, try to fix it without telling others, or lament it to where the mistake is dwelt on past all value. Doesn't handle the mistakes and failures of others well either. | 10. Learn to admit mistakes, warn those affected, learn from them, and move on to something else. It's relatively easy to find scapegoats, or to simply not think much about our blunders, or to naively believe it will never happen again. Learning from hardship situations requires looking inside and thinking about how to respond better to avoid being blindsided as often in the future. |

A development-in-place system can help with today's issues of dual-career couples, "downsizing," those who wish challenge more than advancement, and can help season those for whom advancement is important.

Finally, a checklist for setting up a system for development in place:

### Setting Up a System for Development in Place

1.   Identify specific assignments in each of the five assignment categories.

2.   Form strategy for matching managers with assignments:
     • Voluntary
     • General
     • Targeted

3.   Form strategy for assisting managers to learn:
     • Specify transitions they are making
     • Plan what they will do differently
     • Plan learning methods they will use

4.   Provide feedback on how effectively they learn:
     • What they are learning
     • Blocks to learning/aids to learning

# References

The Center for Creative Leadership's studies of executive learning from experience began in 1982 and are continuing. Many publications have resulted from these investigations and have been referred to throughout this article.

The technical aspects of the interviews and surveys of key events and lessons are detailed in *Key Events in Executives' Lives* by Esther Lindsey, Virginia Homes, and Morgan McCall. A non-technical depiction of the studies, which contains several implications sections, has been published (*The Lessons of Experience* by Morgan McCall, Michael Lombardo, and Ann Morrison; Lexington Books, 1988). A companion interview study of executive women was published in 1987 by Addison-Wesley (*Breaking the Glass Ceiling: Can Women Reach the Top of America's Largest Corporations?* by Ann Morrison, Randall White, and Ellen Van Velsor). Three studies of derailment—*Off the Track: Why and How Successful Executives Get Derailed* (McCall and Lombardo), *Success and Derailment in Upper-Level Management Positions* (Lombardo, Marian Ruderman, and Cynthia McCauley), and *The Dynamics of Management Derailment* (Lombardo and McCauley)—have been published. A summary and interpretation of the values oriented events, *Values in Action: The Meaning of Executive Vignettes* (Lombardo); a description and interpretation of other research into development experiences for managers, *Developmental Experiences in Managerial Work* (McCauley), and an inventory measuring executive lessons, derailment factors and challenging jobs, *Benchmarks*® (Lombardo and McCauley)—have been published. All are available from the Center for Creative Leadership, Publication, Post Office Box 26300, Greensboro, North Carolina 27438-6300.

Other references we relied on are Thomas Peters, *Thriving on Chaos* (Random House, 1987); and Douglas T. Hall and Samuel Rabinowitz, "Maintaining Employee Involvement in a Plateaued Career," in Manuel London and Edward M. Mone, *Career Growth and Human Resource Strategies* (Quorum Books, 1988).

# CENTER FOR CREATIVE LEADERSHIP PUBLICATIONS

**SELECTED REPORTS:**

**The Adventures of Team Fantastic: A Practical Guide for Team Leaders and Members**
G.L. Hallam (1996, Stock #172) ................................................................................................ $20.00
**Beyond Work-Family Programs** J.R. Kofodimos (1995, Stock #167) ................................................ $15.00
**CEO Selection: A Street-smart Review** G.P. Hollenbeck (1994, Stock #164) .................................... .$25.00
**Choosing 360: A Guide to Evaluating Multi-rater Feedback Instruments for Management**
**Development** E. Van Velsor, J. Brittain Leslie, & J.W. Fleenor (1997, Stock #334) ............................ $15.00
**Creativity in the R&D Laboratory** T.M. Amabile & S.S. Gryskiewicz (1987, Stock #130) ............... $12.00
**Eighty-eight Assignments for Development in Place: Enhancing the Developmental Challenge**
**of Existing Jobs** M.M. Lombardo & R.W. Eichinger (1989, Stock #136) ....................................... $15.00
**Enhancing 360-degree Feedback for Senior Executives: How to Maximize the Benefits and**
**Minimize the Risks** R.E. Kaplan & C.J. Palus (1994, Stock #160) ......................................................... $15.00
**An Evaluation of the Outcomes of a Leadership Development Program** C.D. McCauley &
M.W. Hughes-James (1994, Stock #163) ................................................................................................ $20.00
**Evolving Leaders: A Model for Promoting Leadership Development in Programs** C.J. Palus &
W.H. Drath (1995, Stock #165) ............................................................................................................. $20.00
**Forceful Leadership and Enabling Leadership: You Can Do Both** R.E. Kaplan (1996, Stock #171) $20.00
**Four Essential Ways that Coaching Can Help Executives** R. Witherspoon & R.P. White (1997,
Stock #175)............................................................................................................................................. $10.00
**Gender Differences in the Development of Managers: How Women Managers Learn From**
**Experience** E. Van Velsor & M. W. Hughes (1990, Stock #145) ......................................................... $35.00
**A Glass Ceiling Survey: Benchmarking Barriers and Practices** A.M. Morrison, C.T. Schreiber,
& K.F. Price (1995, Stock #161) ............................................................................................................ $20.00
**Helping Leaders Take Effective Action: A Program Evaluation** D.P. Young & N.M. Dixon
(1996, Stock #174) ................................................................................................................................ $18.00
**How to Design an Effective System for Developing Managers and Executives** M.A. Dalton &
G.P. Hollenbeck (1996, Stock #158) ...................................................................................................... $15.00
**Inside View: A Leader's Observations on Leadership** W.F. Ulmer, Jr. (1997, Stock #176) .............. $12.00
**The Intuitive Pragmatists: Conversations with Chief Executive Officers** J.S. Bruce (1986,
Stock #310) ............................................................................................................................................. $12.00
**Leadership for Turbulent Times** L.R. Sayles (1995, Stock #325) ........................................................ $20.00
**Learning How to Learn From Experience: Impact of Stress and Coping** K.A. Bunker &
A.D. Webb (1992, Stock #154) .............................................................................................................. $30.00
**A Look at Derailment Today: North America and Europe** J. Brittain Leslie & E. Van Velsor
(1996, Stock #169) ................................................................................................................................ $25.00
**Making Common Sense: Leadership as Meaning-making in a Community of Practice**
W.H. Drath & C.J. Palus (1994, Stock #156) ....................................................................................... $15.00
**Managerial Promotion: The Dynamics for Men and Women** M.N. Ruderman, P.J. Ohlott, &
K.E. Kram (1996, Stock #170) .............................................................................................................. $15.00
**Managing Across Cultures: A Learning Framework** M.S. Wilson, M.H. Hoppe, & L.R. Sayles
(1996, Stock #173) ................................................................................................................................ $15.00
**Off the Track: Why and How Successful Executives Get Derailed** M.W. McCall, Jr., &
M.M. Lombardo (1983, Stock #121) ..................................................................................................... $10.00
**Perspectives on Dialogue: Making Talk Developmental for Individuals and Organizations**
N.M. Dixon (1996, Stock #168) ............................................................................................................ $20.00
**Preventing Derailment: What To Do Before It's Too Late** M.M. Lombardo & R.W. Eichinger
(1989, Stock #138) ................................................................................................................................ $25.00
**The Realities of Management Promotion** M.N. Ruderman & P.J. Ohlott (1994, Stock #157) ............ $15.00
**Selection at the Top: An Annotated Bibliography** V.I. Sessa & R.J. Campbell (1997, Stock #333)... $20.00
**Succession Planning: An Annotated Bibliography** L.J. Eastman (1995, Stock #324) ........................ $20.00
**Training for Action: A New Approach to Executive Development** R.M. Burnside &
V.A. Guthrie (1992, Stock #153) ........................................................................................................... $15.00
**Traps and Pitfalls in the Judgment of Executive Potential** M.N. Ruderman & P.J. Ohlott
(1990, Stock #141) ................................................................................................................................ $20.00
**Twenty-two Ways to Develop Leadership in Staff Managers** R.W. Eichinger & M.M. Lombardo
(1990, Stock #144) ................................................................................................................................ $15.00
**Using an Art Technique to Facilitate Leadership Development** C. De Ciantis (1995, Stock #166)... $20.00
**Why Managers Have Trouble Empowering: A Theoretical Perspective Based on Concepts of**
**Adult Development** W.H. Drath (1993, Stock #155) ......................................................................... $15.00

## SELECTED BOOKS:

**Balancing Act: How Managers Can Integrate Successful Careers and Fulfilling Personal Lives**
J.R. Kofodimos (1993, Stock #247) .................................................................................................. $27.00

**Beyond Ambition: How Driven Managers Can Lead Better and Live Better** R.E. Kaplan,
W.H. Drath, & J.R. Kofodimos (1991, Stock #227) ........................................................................ $29.95

**Breaking the Glass Ceiling: Can Women Reach the Top of America's Largest Corporations?**
**(Updated Edition)** A.M. Morrison, R.P. White, & E. Van Velsor (1992, Stock #236A) .................... $13.00

**Choosing to Lead (Second Edition)** K.E. Clark & M.B. Clark (1996, Stock #327) ........................... $25.00

**Developing Diversity in Organizations: A Digest of Selected Literature** A.M. Morrison &
K.M. Crabtree (1992, Stock #317) ................................................................................................. $25.00

**Discovering Creativity: Proceedings of the 1992 International Creativity and Innovation**
**Networking Conference** S.S. Gryskiewicz (Ed.) (1993, Stock #319) ................................................. $30.00

**Executive Selection: A Look at What We Know and What We Need to Know** D.L. DeVries
(1993, Stock #321) ......................................................................................................................... $20.00

**Healing the Wounds: Overcoming the Trauma of Layoffs and Revitalizing Downsized**
**Organizations** D.M. Noer (1993, Stock #245) ............................................................................... $28.50

**If I'm In Charge Here, Why Is Everybody Laughing?** D.P. Campbell (1984, Stock #205) ................ $8.95

**If You Don't Know Where You're Going You'll Probably End Up Somewhere Else**
D.P. Campbell (1974, Stock #203) ................................................................................................... $9.95

**Inklings: Collected Columns on Leadership and Creativity** D.P. Campbell (1992, Stock #233) ....... $15.00

**Leadership Education 1996-1997: A Source Book (Sixth Edition), Vol. 1, Courses and**
**Programs** F.H. Freeman, K.B. Knott, & M.K. Schwartz (Eds.) (1996, Stock #330) ............................. $35.00

**Leadership Education 1996-1997: A Source Book (Sixth Edition), Vol. 2, Leadership Resources**
F.H. Freeman, K.B. Knott, & M.K. Schwartz (Eds.) (1996, Stock #331) .............................................. $35.00

**Leadership: Enhancing the Lessons of Experience (Second Edition)** R.L. Hughes, R.C. Ginnett,
& G.J. Curphy (1996, Stock #266) ................................................................................................... $49.95

**The Lessons of Experience: How Successful Executives Develop on the Job** M.W. McCall, Jr.,
M.M. Lombardo, & A.M. Morrison (1988, Stock #211) ..................................................................... $22.95

**Making Diversity Happen: Controversies and Solutions** A.M. Morrison, M.N. Ruderman, &
M. Hughes-James (1993, Stock #320) .............................................................................................. $25.00

**The New Leaders: Guidelines on Leadership Diversity in America** A.M. Morrison (1992,
Stock #238) .................................................................................................................................... $29.00

**Readings in Innovation** S.S. Gryskiewicz & D.A. Hills (Eds.) (1992, Stock #240) ............................ $25.00

**Selected Research on Work Team Diversity** M.N. Ruderman, M.W. Hughes-James, &
S.E. Jackson (Eds.) (1996, Stock #326) ........................................................................................... $24.95

**Take the Road to Creativity and Get Off Your Dead End** D.P. Campbell (1977, Stock #204) ........... $8.95

**The Working Leader: The Triumph of High Performance Over Conventional Management**
**Principles** L.R. Sayles (1993, Stock #243) ...................................................................................... $27.95

## SPECIAL PACKAGES:

**Development and Derailment** (Stock #702; includes 136, 138, & 144) .............................................. $35.00

**The Diversity Collection** (Stock #708; includes 145, 236A, 238, 317, & 320) .................................... $85.00

**Executive Selection** (Stock #710; includes 141, 321, & 157) .......................................................... $32.00

**Gender Research** (Stock #716; includes 145, 161, 170, 236, 238, & 317) ........................................ $90.00

**HR Professional's Info Pack** (Stock #717; includes 136, 158, 165, 169, 324, & 334) ....................... $75.00

**Leadership Education 1996-1997: A Source Book—Volumes 1 & 2** (Stock #714; includes 330
& 331) ............................................................................................................................................ $60.00

**New Understanding of Leadership** (Stock #718; includes 156, 165, & 168) ..................................... $40.00

**Personal Growth, Taking Charge, and Enhancing Creativity** (Stock #231; includes 203, 204,
& 205) ............................................................................................................................................ $20.00

Discounts are available. Please write for a comprehensive Publications catalog. Address your request to: Publication, Center for Creative Leadership, P.O. Box 26300, Greensboro, NC 27438-6300, 910-545-2805, or fax to 910-545-3221. All prices subject to change.

# ORDER FORM

Name _____ Title _____

Organization _____

Mailing Address _____
(street address required for mailing)

City/State/Zip _____

Telephone _____ FAX _____
(telephone number required for UPS mailing)

| Quantity | Stock No. | Title | Unit Cost | Amount |
|---|---|---|---|---|
|  |  |  |  |  |
|  |  |  |  |  |
|  |  |  |  |  |
|  |  |  |  |  |
|  |  |  |  |  |
|  |  |  |  |  |
|  |  |  |  |  |
|  |  |  |  |  |
|  |  |  |  |  |

CCL's Federal ID Number
is 237-07-9591.

| | |
|---|---|
| **Subtotal** | |
| **Shipping and Handling** (add 6% of subtotal with a $4.00 minimum; add 40% on all international shipping) | |
| NC residents add 6% sales tax; CA residents add 7.75% sales tax; CO residents add 6% sales tax | |
| **TOTAL** | |

**METHOD OF PAYMENT**
**(ALL orders for less than $100 must be PREPAID.)**

❏ Check or money order enclosed (payable to Center for Creative Leadership).

❏ Purchase Order No. _____ (Must be accompanied by this form.)

❏ Charge my order, plus shipping, to my credit card:
        ❏ American Express  ❏ Discover  ❏ MasterCard  ❏ VISA

ACCOUNT NUMBER:_____ EXPIRATION DATE: MO.____ YR.____

NAME OF ISSUING BANK: _____

SIGNATURE _____

❏ Please put me on your mailing list.

**Publication • Center for Creative Leadership • P.O. Box 26300**
**Greensboro, NC 27438-6300**
**910-545-2805 • FAX 910-545-3221**

Client Priority Code: R

fold here

**CENTER FOR CREATIVE LEADERSHIP**
PUBLICATION
P.O. Box 26300
Greensboro, NC 27438-6300